GRAND

Mesa

COUNTRY

*Stories from
Mesa & Delta Counties
in Colorado*

BY ABBOTT FAY

WESTERN REFLECTIONS PUBLISHING COMPANY

Montrose, CO

All photos by author unless noted.

ISBN-13: 978-1-932738-22-3
ISBN-10: 1-932738-22-3

Library of Congress Control Number: 2005921299

Cover and text design: Laurie Goralka Design

First Edition
Printed in the United States of America

Western Reflections Publishing Company®
219 Main Street
Montrose, CO 81401
www.westernreflectionspub.com

Colorado Books by Abbott Fay:

Mountain Academia
Ski Tracks in the Rockies
Famous Coloradans
I Never Knew That About Colorado
Beyond the Great Divide
More That I Never Knew About Colorado
To Think That This Happened in Grand County!
A History of Skiing in Colorado
The Story of Colorado Wines
Grand Mesa Country

WHAT THIS IS MOSTLY ABOUT

- It's mostly about common people with a few uncommon ones thrown in.

- It's about true stories, or else legends, some truly believed.

- It's about two counties in western Colorado where anyone can look up and see Grand Mesa, also called Thunder Mountain.

- It's about Native Americans, explorers, town-founders, orchardists, vintners, scientists, teachers, craftsmen, artists, writers, horse traders, lawyers, doctors, morticians, clergymen, entrepreneurs, offbeat characters, outlaws and even politicians.

- It's about stories that have almost been forgotten, but should not be forgotten.

TABLE OF CONTENTS

The Land and Its Discoverers

Mines and Miners

Trees, Fruits, and Veggies

The Land
and its
Discoverers

A UTE LEGEND OF
THUNDER MOUNTAIN

Once it was Called Thigunawat

Grand Mesa, the 10,000+ foot mountain that looms over the Grand Valley, was known by several different names in the pre-history of the Ute Indians. It was called Thigunawat, which meant "home of departed spirits," by the earliest Indians; a later name, according to tribal elders, was Thunder Mountain, recalling the legend of the "thunderbirds" or mythic eagles, which were said to nest along the rim of the plateau and create fearful lightning storms.

The legend of the thunderbirds tells that there were three pairs of great eagles, known as Bahaa-Niehe. The white rockslides on the slopes of Grand Mesa were said to be formed by bones from their nests. One day a Bahaa-Niehe seized the son of Sehiwaq, a Ute tribal leader, and carried the infant to its nest for a meal. Bent on revenge, Sehiwaq wrapped himself in the bark of red cedar and climbed all day to the top of the mountain. Whenever a thunderbird would fly near, the Ute leader stood still, pretending to be a tree. He finally reached the nests and pulled out the young birds, flinging them down the side of the mountain. The huge serpent, Batiqtuba, who lived at the foot of the slope, devoured the young eagles at once. When the Bahaa-Niehe returned to their empty nests, they assumed the serpent had made the raid, so they attacked him, carried him into the sky and tore him to pieces. As the pieces fell to earth they formed great pits, which soon filled with water to become a hundred lakes. The Bahaa-Niehe never discovered that Sehiwaq was the raider of the nest.

There came a period when the Utes considered the Mesa a scared place, home to departed spirits, and henceforth did not climb to the top, except during the ritual for an adolescent boy to be initiated into manhood. The boy would be instructed to climb to the highest point along the edge, with no food, water, or weapons. There he was to await a message from his ancestors. When he perceived the message — usually an omen of the future — he would return and tell the tribal members. That was his passage into manhood with all its respects and privileges, including marriage. If there was no message, he was never to return. According to the Utes who told of this ritual, almost every boy returned. Hunger consistently opens the doors of perception, they noted.

THE OOZE AND FLOW OF BASALT

Volcanic Capping of Grand Mesa

During the last major Rocky Mountain uplift, about fifteen million years ago, volcanic explosions flowed westward from what are now called the Elk and West Elk Ranges. The remaining underground lava seeped through fissures in the basalt and created molten stone. It is estimated that during the last ten million years, there were at least nine different ejections, flowing out to form a cap of hard stone 200 to 300 feet thick. Leon Park on Grand Mesa, at 11,234 feet above sea level, is thought to be the greatest source of these eruptions.

As normal erosion gradually carved out the softer sides beyond the flow, Grand Mesa held fast, creating what are now the Colorado and Gunnison Valleys. Through the eons of geologic time, nature provided soil with decomposition and dust, giving a lush foundation for vegetation and more than 200 ponds. The resulting elevation change between the high crest and the low desert lands has given Delta and Mesa Counties a delightful contrast in climate. The volcanic rock has also provided beautiful stone for churches and other buildings in Eckert and Cedaredge.

4   *Cedaredge Church built of Grand Mesa lava flow.*

WEIRD FORMATIONS

Arches, Hoodoos, and a Miracle Rock

There are a number of rather interesting land formations in Mesa County.

Most numerous are those called "hoodoos," or when massed together, "goblins." The largest gathering of goblins, with human-like shapes, is about twenty-nine miles west of DeBeque, in the wild horse country. These spooky formations are all over the canyons at the southern foot of Mount Garfield, and under a full moon they cast eerie shadows on the surrounding landscape.

In Rattlesnake Canyon, almost on the Utah border, there are at least twelve natural arches in the sandstone. The largest is 120 feet high and 8 feet across and is accessible by a long hike. Another arch can be reached by four-wheel drive on a road south of Colorado National Monument.

Miracle Rock — eighty-five feet high, one-foot sandstone base.

Photo by Frank Carr

5

These arches form the largest concentration anywhere on the continent except for Arches National Park, about fifty miles west in Utah.

The best-known balanced rock in the area is near the west entrance of Colorado National Monument, but a more precariously teetering one is Miracle Rock in Glade Park. It is estimated to be a 12,000-ton boulder, ninety-five feet tall, and balanced on a one-foot wide ridge. This is as tall as a nine-story building! This rock overlooks a cliff 200 feet deep, and some have claimed that this is the largest balanced rock in the world. It is well worth the effort to see this formation, and it can be found 14.9 miles west of the Glade Park store.

WHAT RIGGS DUG UP

An Eighteen-Foot Forelimb

It was not unusual for area ranchers to collect the dinosaur bones they found in the early days of this region. In 1899, one prospector, a Grand Junction dentist named Dr. S.M. Bradbury, realized that the bones may have unique interest. He sent a letter to Chicago's Field Museum of Natural History and suggested there might be remains of large dinosaurs in Mesa County. It attracted the attention of Elmer Riggs, assistant curator of paleontology, who decided to board a train the next year and come to Grand Junction for a look-see.

Riggs found a bone eighteen feet in length on a mound in the Redlands area south of town. This was the forearm of a

Museum of Western Colorado volunteers work to unearth the Bollan Stegosaurus near Rabbit Valley, Colorado.
Gretel Daugherty photograph, Loyd Files Research Library, Museum of Western Colorado.

brachiosaurus, the largest land animal ever known at that time. It has since been determined that the giant lived 150 million years ago. Most of the other bones were excavated and reconstructed later at the Chicago Museum, where they became an exhibit, which attracted worldwide attention.

RIVERA GOT TO PURGATORY

It Was in Delta County

In the first systematic exploration of western Colorado, Spanish priests Francisco Atanasio Dominguez and Silvestre Velez de Escalante arrived near the confluence of the Uncompahgre and Gunnison Rivers on August 27, 1776. They found a tree which had been marked with a cross eleven years earlier by Juan Maria de Rivera. The inscription read: "Viva Jesus," with Rivera's name, and the date of November 20, 1765. It is now known that he called the place "El Purgatorio."

Rivera was searching for silver and also looking for the "Rio del Tizon," which was the name for what is now the Colorado River. When he arrived at El Purgatorio, he apparently believed he had found the Colorado River, rather than the Gunnison.

This realization has come to light as a result of the accidental discovery in 1990 of a journal of Rivera's travels. Dr. Don Cutter of Albuquerque, New Mexico, was studying archives in Spain when he came across the document. While it was not exacting in site identification, it was the first explanation of Rivera's journey through this region and proved that Dominguez and Escalante followed the same general route as Rivera. Steve Baker, of Centuries Research in Montrose, Colorado, worked with Cutter in the translation and re-tracing of the Rivera expedition. Before Cutter's find, historians had given up hope that any record of Rivera's travels would be located.

MARRYING THE GOVERNOR'S DAUGHTER

A Bonanza for Antoine Robidoux

Antoine Robidoux, born in 1795, was one of six brothers from St. Louis who became noted throughout the West in the fur trade. After the eldest brother, Joseph, founded St. Joseph in Missouri, Antoine went to Santa Fe, in what was then Mexico.

In 1824, he was one of a group who crossed the Continental Divide in Colorado and explored north to what later became Wyoming Territory. The American Fur Company dominated that region, and the Mexicans resented their intrusions into Utah and Idaho, which were part of the original Spanish conquest claims. The region was rich in beaver and other fur-bearing animals.

Mexico enacted a law allowing only its citizens to trade or trap in the lands west and north of Santa Fe. Antoine applied for and was granted Mexican citizenship. He was very popular in Santa Fe and became a member of the city council there. He also fell in love with Carmel Benevides, adopted daughter of the Mexican governor. The governor gave Antoine permission to marry the adventurous sixteen-year-old in 1828.

That same year, Antoine was given an exclusive license to establish trade in the western Colorado and eastern Utah regions. His party has been credited as the first to cross the Continental Divide at Cochetopa Pass in Colorado with a wagon. He may have reached as far as the modern town of Gunnison with wagons or carts, but, from there, the land either north or south of the Gunnison River was so rugged that only pack animals could be used. Following the south side of the Black Canyon, he finally reached the confluence of the Uncompahgre River with the Gunnison, and there established the first of three trading forts from which he would build his trading empire, Fort Uncompahgre, in what is now Delta County.

The fort flourished from 1828 until 1844, when Mexicans at Santa Fe attacked Ute Indians. The intended target was the Navajo Nation, but they did not make a distinction between the tribes. The word spread northward and put the Utes on the warpath. They destroyed the fort, leaving only one man alive. Robidoux was in Utah at the time of the attack and heard of the destruction of his fort from the sole survivor. Antoine and Carmel then returned to Missouri, where he died in 1860. Although the exact location is not known, the fort has been reconstructed as a living history museum in Delta and is now a popular attraction for tourists and history buffs.

NAMING THE BOOK CLIFFS

Who First Thought They Looked Like Books?

The Book Cliffs loom over the Grand Valley in a stunning forma-tion. Sometimes the name appears in accounts as two words, "Book Cliffs," and sometimes as the "Bookcliff Range," or just "Bookcliffs." John Williams Gunnison explored the area in 1853, and his topog-rapher, Richard H. Kern, marked the formation as the "Roan or Book Mountains." This is believed to be the first mention of the word "book" to describe the range.

John Wesley Powell's account of his epic trip by boat down the Green and Colorado Rivers in 1869 also referred to the "Book Cliffs." In 1875-1876, F.V. Hayden headed the first scientific survey to map the region. His topographer, Henry Garnet, used the terms "Roan" and "Book" cliffs, noting that the first term referred to color and second to resemblance of a series of upright books on a shelf.

Geologist William L. Chenowith wrote, "Today, persons look-ing at the Book Cliffs see either books upright or open, or lying on their sides, or a stack of books, or no books at all, and the 1853 ori-gin of the name is still unclear."

NORTH BRANCH OF
THE OLD SPANISH TRAIL

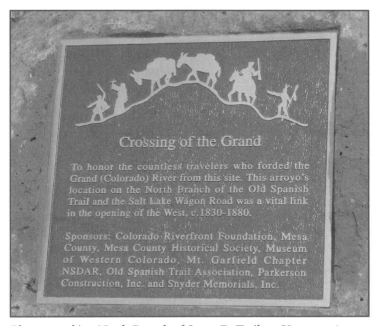

*A Gulch Off Today's
Unaweep Avenue*

On Unaweep Avenue in Grand Junction, where 28¼ Road would be if it continued south of the Colorado River, there is an overgrown gulch. It leads down to the river and has a rich history as the most-used place for crossing the river on the North Branch of the Old Spanish Trail and the later Salt Lake Wagon Route. There is now a

Plaque marking North Branch of Sante Fe Trail on Unaweep Avenue in Grand Junction.

Photo by Randy Fay

stone marker on the north side of Unaweep Avenue. Through this gully traveled many illustrious figures of the American West.

Antoine Robidoux, founder of Fort Uncompahgre near Delta, crossed the river here to explore and later build Fort Uintah in Utah. Christopher "Kit" Carson made the crossing at least two times. Rufus Sage, whose 1846 book, *Scenes in the Rocky Mountains,* became a classic in its field, crossed there in 1842. Missionary Doctor Marcus Whitman made the journey from his Oregon mission to Taos, New Mexico, fording the Colorado River in 1842. John Williams Gunnison's expedition, searching for a transcontinental railroad route in 1853, probably also used the crossing.

In 1853, Lt. Edward Beale described the crossing at this spot in his notes. Beale became controversial three years later, when, as Brigadier General of the California Militia, he formed a camel corps for transportation across the southwest deserts. F.V. Hayden led the first scientific survey of western Colorado in 1874 and 1875. It was the Hayden crew that named many places in the region. Crossing the river at this point with him was the most famous of the pioneer photographers of the West, William Henry Jackson. They were headed northward toward Yellowstone in Wyoming.

THE DESERT DIDN'T STINK

Escalante Never Even Saw It

According to a myth created by a Grand Junction businessman, explorer Escalante in 1776 described the region between present-day Delta and Grand Junction as "the stinking desert." Escalante and Dominguez never saw this region, having turned eastward before reaching it and crossing Grand Mesa north of Paonia. The canyons named for the explorers do exist there, named on a presumption that they should have continued on that route. There is nothing "stinking" about the region, which is more attractive than many other deserts.

Escalante Mural, Paonia. Mural by Ginny Allen

HOW OTTO MEARS
CHEATED THE UTES

$2,800 for Eleven Million Acres

Famed "road builder of the San Juans," Otto Mears, was appointed to negotiate a "buy out" with the Ute Indians during their evacuation from western Colorado. The U.S. Government was confident that the Utes would welcome yearly interest on $1,800,000. That price represented about $1.70 per acre on eleven million acres of land and encompassed much of what is now western Colorado, including Mesa and Delta Counties. The yearly interest for the tribe would have come to about $54,000.

Mears agreed to give each of the male Utes two dollars as an inducement to sign the treaty. The total paid was only $2,800. When he was accused of bribery, Mears defended his deal by explaining that the Utes preferred a small cash settlement to an uncertain interest payment. The delighted federal government was quick to refund his expenditures.

Mines

and

Miners

COAL, COPPER, AND ALABASTER

Plus the Collbran Gold Rush

While the production of uranium and vanadium in Mesa County was much publicized, it was coal that was the most important mineral, as well as in Delta County. Along the Bookcliffs there were at least twenty-seven coal mines at one time or another.

The town of Carpenter, north of today's Walker Field, had its own railroad, the Little Bookcliff narrow-gauge line. The Gerhart Mine on Mount Lincoln above Palisade was remembered for its policy of allowing the poor to pick through its slag pile for usable coal. So-called "farmers' mines," in which labor was donated and coal was free, existed above Fruita and Hotchkiss. The whole town of Cameo was based on coal production and the electric power it produced. At Cedaredge there were several mines, in one of which a gigantic dinosaur track was found. The longest lasting coal mines were near Paonia, which continue to send out hundreds of railroad carloads of coal a day.

Copper was the main product of at least nine mines in the Unaweep Canyon region. Two mostly-tent "cities," Pearl City and Copper City, existed there between 1893 and 1912, along with a smelter. There were also small bits of gold and some gem-quality amethyst produced. Orren (Ike) Hubbard produced building blocks of alabaster from a canyon near Gateway.

Several attempts to drill for oil were made near the towns of Austin and Paonia in Delta County, but the efforts did not prove profitable. Oil shale was known to exist near DeBeque as early as World War I, but the process for profitable commercial production never materialized.

Gold flakes were found in several streams, but never any large quantity, which led to the following account in *The Mining and Scientific Press* of 1913 that described the "rush" to Clover Gulch and Kimball Creek northwest of Collbran.

A rush to the recent gold discoveries near Collbran has started from all parts of the state. Scores of men are coming in from DeBeque on every stage and the mining camp in Clover Gulch is taking on the appearance of a tented city. Over 150 claims have already been staked, and the claims extend for 14 miles up and down Clover Gulch, while prospectors are now staking other claims on Kimball Creek. The advance prospectors from the Eagle district report that they will be followed by scores of other prospectors if early reports of discoveries are borne out. Additional assays of ore have been made and show from $138 to $150 per ton, with indications of a streak of uranium. Merchants of Collbran have ordered large quantities of tents and other camp supplies.

Actually, Clover Gulch is only about two miles long. If there was any local excitement over gold, it must have vanished overnight!

MINER, COBBLER, AND DAIRYMAN

The Trials and Triumphs of Clement Auden

Clement Auden was born in 1879 in Belgium, and, by the age of eleven, began working in the local coal mines fourteen hours a day, six days a week, for eighteen cents a day. He hand-sorted the coal and his efficiency was so noted that he was given a raise to seventy cents a day by the next year.

In 1903, he met and married his wife, Rosa. Promises of the good life in America inspired Clement to borrow ten dollars from his mother to migrate to the United States. He went to Danville, Illinois, and became a coal miner. By 1908, he had saved enough money to enable Rosa to join him in Illinois. They moved that year to Somerset, Colorado, where Clement found work for Utah Fuel Company at three dollars a day.

They were living in Somerset when their firstborn son, two-and-a-half year old Paul, became very ill with pneumonia. Asked what he most wanted, Paul replied that he would like a cow. Clement went out, bought a cow, and brought it home. He held Paul up to the window to see the cow grazing in the yard. The child was thrilled and died a few moments later with a smile on his little face. Following the death of Paul, the superintendent of the mine told him he could not keep a cow in Somerset, so the Audens moved east of town, where they started a dairy farm.

Clement continued working for the mine, returning each night to pitch hay. He also realized he had a penchant for shoe repair and spent many winter nights applying new soles for miners' worn-out shoes. With his various ventures, Auden was able to save $2,500 over the course of eighteen months, enough to buy a 160-acre ranch along the North Fork of the Gunnison River.

Rosa gave birth to three more sons and two daughters. Clement and her would rise at 4:00 a.m. to milk the cows while the children, as they grew old enough, would deliver the milk in town before going to school. Clement repaired all the shoes of his fellow miners and continued to ride into the mine on his horse to work a full shift every day.

In 1932, Clement founded the Hawks Nest coal mine, which supplied coal to the railroad and other industries and homes. It was a great success, and he was saluted nationally by the DuPont Corporation, as well as other organizations. Finally feeling his age, Clement sold his interest to his three sons, Abel, Clement Jr., and Ralph, in 1954. He died in 1957. The mine was eventually sold to the Champion Coal Company. Abel retired in 1970 in ill health. Clement Jr. was fatally injured in an accident outside the mine in 1973, and Ralph died in 1974. Thus ended a great family saga in the history of North Fork mining history.

THE OLD GILSONITE REFINERY

A Forty-Niner Prospected
an Ant Hill

As of this writing, the old gilsonite refinery west of Fruita is still rusting away. The sheer cost of reclaiming the polluted soil makes it a white elephant on the real estate market. Around 1850, Samuel H. Gilson, either bound for or returning from the gold fields of California, found himself observing an anthill in the Uintah Basin, north of the Bookcliff Range. He noticed pieces of shiny black mineral being toted by the ants. Digging down, he found the vein of a mineral, which would later bear his name.

This discovery was reported in St. Louis newspapers and caught the interest of engineer C.O. Baxter. The two men experimented with the mineral and soon found it to be a substitute for asphalt. St. Louis brewer Busch was convinced this would be an inexpensive material for lining beer kegs, rather than the asphalt being imported from Sicily for that purpose.

Remains of Gilsonite Refinery.

Photo by Frank Carr

Gilson and Baxter founded the St. Louis Gilsonite Company and filed claims in the Uintah Basin, the world's largest and most concentrated source of solid petroleum, which is almost as light as water. By 1887, they built a refinery in Illinois, which was later purchased by the Barber Asphaltium Corporation. It produced the varnish for Henry Ford's paint on the Model T car and was also used on Lindbergh's "Spirit of St. Louis" for his famous solo flight across the Atlantic. Gilsonite provided protective cover for the Transatlantic Cable and also was used in the production of printers' ink, brake linings, blasting agents, oil well cement, and soundproofing, as well as dozens of other uses.

It was in 1903 that John M. Mack, president of the company, decided on a more efficient method of transporting the product from the Bonanza, Utah, mines to the railroad in the Grand Valley. Thus was developed the Uintah Railroad, a narrow-gauge system often called "the crookedest railway in the United States." It consisted of fifty-three miles of track, crossed seventy-five bridges, and went over 8,500-foot-altitude Baxter Pass. It had steep grades and very sharp curves.

The railroad was not abandoned until 1957, when truck transportation proved more efficient. That same year, work began on a pipeline that would transport the mineral in water to a new refinery, two miles west of Fruita. Mergers formed what came to be known as the American Gilsonite Company. The slurry pipeline carried 1,500 tons of gilsonite in 240,000 gallons of water at about three miles an hour. It took about 24 hours for the mineral to reach the refinery from Bonanza.

Among other products, the refinery produced gasoline, selling to various companies such as Chevron, on the Western Slope. Many Grand Valley cars were supplied with gilsonite fuel. Competitive sources of gasoline production caused gilsonite fuel production to become unprofitable, and the refinery converted to oil processing. Since smoke pollution covered much of the lower valley, and costs outran prices, the refinery was abandoned in the latter days of the Twentieth Century. The refinery remains an eyesore on the landscape, but no longer pollutes the air.

WHEN THE BOWIE MINE
MOVED TO DENVER

It Flew Part Way by Helicopter

One of the most impressive displays at the Colorado History Museum in the Denver Civic Center is the equipment used for some seven decades at the Bowie Coal Mine. The mine entrance itself was high above the North Fork of the Gunnison River, about five miles east of Paonia.

One can now view the sections of the tipple, with its huge rotary dump, gear shaft, and braking mechanism. They hold a commanding position on the basement level of the museum, with expert explanations of their use. They are a tribute to coal mining in Colorado and throughout the West.

In 1981, Coors Energy Corporation donated the equipment to the historical society. Tom Rick, a millwright from upstate New York, was put in charge of the huge task of moving the equipment from its precarious perch. By July and August of 1982, the work was under way. Chinook helicopters from Fort Carson would lift such items as the blower fan, which had been cut into four sections, and circle around to leave them next to Highway 133, where flatbed trucks awaited them. There was also the giant steam engine which had to be lifted out of its setting and a coal loader which was dragged down a dirt road.

When the flatbed trucks reached downtown Denver, a new problem presented itself. The loading dock for the museum was too small for the huge trucks and the ramp to the dock had a turn in it, which meant that a smaller vehicle would have to carry the machinery into the museum.

As David Wetzel, who was later in charge of the historical society publications, remembered it, the equipment had to be placed on "crawlers," and some twenty people walked it down the route to its current and, it is hoped, final resting place.

Trees, fruits, and vegies

THREE OF COLORADO'S
LARGEST TREES

All in Cedaredge

In 1995, the Colorado Forest Service announced that three Cedaredge trees were the largest of their species in the state. They are the horse chestnut at 535 E. 2nd Street, the pine oak at 105 N. 5th Street, and the white ash at 210 Aspen. With the presentation of these awards, the town was designated as "Tree City USA."

Largest horse chestnut tree in Colorado. Cedaredge.

THE GRAND VALLEY'S FIRST
SUCCESSFUL PEACH ORCHARD

Harlow's Rapid Creek Farm

John Petal (J.P.) Harlow, a Canadian by birth, was living with his wife, Kate, in Gunnison when the Utes were removed and the Grand Valley opened for settlement in 1881. John and Kate came to Grand Junction in December of that year, building a house on Rapid Creek and another in what became the town of Palisade. Kate opened a restaurant in Grand Junction, and John planted vegetables and fruit trees at Rapid Creek. The farm did well, supplying Kate with fresh produce for her dining establishment. The fruit trees, however, died, but John re-planted, using "burnt bones and leached ashes" to fertilize the soil.

By 1886, John's orchards bore their first fruits, including superb peaches. In 1887, he had what may have been the first successful crop of peaches in Colorado. They won blue ribbons at a Denver exhibition, and John later gave a talk at the first horticultural society meeting in Grand Junction, explaining soil treatment and urging farmers to grow peaches. John supplemented their income by serving as a U.S. Marshall and also entered into partnership with Grand Junction founder George Crawford in the development of a coal mine on the farm.

When Harlow passed away in 1895, at the age of sixty-one, he was interred at the farm. His gravestone still stands among trees on the Rapid Creek Road, near the stonewalls of his house, which are possibly the oldest surviving ruins of a residence in the Grand Valley.

WHERE DID THE GLOBE WILLOWS COME FROM?

None Were Here Before World War II

Visitors to the Grand Valley and Delta County and as far as the North Fork of the Gunnison River are often attracted to the globe willow trees, which grow only in favored areas. With their almost geometrically-perfect global dimensions, they can be torn apart by heavy snowfall — luckily a rare occurrence in this region. They also thrive in arid climates, are among the first to leaf out in the late winter, and among the last to lose their leaves in the fall. They are popular landscaping touches, providing welcome shade.

Fruita historian Yvonne Peterson decided to check out the origin of the globe willows in the Grand Valley. The story goes back to the Potsdam Conference held in the recently defeated Germany in

The Globe Willow arrived after World War II.

Photo by Randy Fay

July of 1945. The liberated nation of Korea, which had been taken over by Japan, was divided at the 38th parallel, and Russian troops occupied North Korea, while the United States troops occupied South Korea.

It was in a section of South Korea that these beautifully-shaped "Chinese willows" were growing. An Army soldier from Texas was so impressed by them that he decided to bring home a globe willow sapling when his tour of duty ended, sometime between 1947 and 1948. It was planted and grew in an arid region in west Texas.

Shortly after that, relatives of Nettie and John Brach, farmers who lived near Fruita, brought a few cuttings from Texas, which later became known as the "globe willow." Planted on the Brach farm, three sticks took root, one of which developed well and grew quickly. That tree became the ancestor of all the other globe willows in this region.

The accuracy of this story is further verified by the lack of any photographic evidence of any globe willows in the Grand Valley prior to or during World War II.

CREATIVE INVENTIONS

Improving the Fruit Industry

J.C. Plank of Grand Junction invented a new and more efficient smudge pot for staving off late freezes in the orchards in 1908. There were two models: one for crude oil and another for coal burning. They were more effective and inexpensive than the California pots that had been in use.

Palisade grower Raymond Peeples invented an electrical peach de-fuzzer, which was produced in a factory in Palisade and used in other peach-growing states.

In 1915, Nancy Bowman of Palisade designed a new style of fruit picking sack. She made a small model of it with a hairpin and handkerchief. Her husband, George, patented the design, and it was a huge success—there were so many orders that they built a factory in Palisade for its manufacture. It was said to be used in almost all fruit-growing areas. George Bowman later organized the United Fruit Growers Association and served as president of the Palisade National Bank for thirty years.

Billy Edwards of Palisade devised a mechanical grader, which sorted fruit into different sizes. The Edwards Grader could then fill each box or basket with products of uniform size.

In 1925, E.B. Hiatt of Palisade devised a mechanical device for "facing peaches when packed in bushels." The Hiatt Pack machine saved much time in arranging the fruits.

Further improvements in the packing and shipping of peaches emerged in 1922 at the Palisade Peach Growers Association packinghouse with the introduction of G.B. Forgman's novel grading system. All peaches were dumped into a well-padded hopper, which then sorted them into four sizes: good, choice, fancy, and extra-fancy. A canvas tube carried each grade to the weighing machine and then by belt to the packing tables where nailers fitted the boxes for

shipping. The process saved the labor of twenty people. Sixty pack-
ers could each prepare 150 boxes a day. The average output for the
day was nine carloads, but that doubled using three expert box-
makers working around the clock. Incidentally, the workers packing
the peaches were mostly women who made over five dollars for a
ten-hour day — considered very good wages at the time.

*Palisade Fruit Growers developed stilt walking to a new height to prune
trees. They marched in the Lions' Convention Parades in Chicago and
New York City.*

Courtesy of Gary Granat

THE GREAT SMOKE-IN

Burn Garbage All Night

Smudge pots were the only protection orchards had for staving off untimely freezes in the earlier days. When a late freeze threatened most of the fruit trees in the Grand Valley in the spring of 1926, the mayor of Grand Junction called for all the people in the valley to burn all the trash they could find late at night. They were to keep the fires burning as smoky as possible all night so as to cover the whole valley with smoke. Thousands of people got into the spirit, often making parties of the event. Most of the fruit was saved, although skeptics claimed the temperature never reached the killing level.

THE SEEDLESS APPLE BUBBLE

Did King Edward VII Say "Best Apple I Ever Tasted?"

In 1905, the Spencer Seedless Apple Company was formed in Grand Junction, starting a nursery with five budded parent trees. These were touted as the apple of the future, with no seeds and from which the pithy core had "practically been eliminated."

Stock in the company was promoted in the eastern states, and the capital poured in. The company claimed it had sent four apples to King Edward VII of Great Britain, and it was reported that His Majesty ate one and pronounced it "Delicious—the best apple I have ever tasted." The other three were auctioned for sixty shillings each.

It was announced that two thousand trees were established, and estimates were that the orchard would furnish two million trees in nursery stock. Each was to sell for two dollars, and stockholders would become wealthy within a year.

However, the reality was that only one tree produced any seedless fruit, and the apples were of poor quality and flavorless. So there was no chance of any commercial success. According to Alvin T. Steinel in *History of Agriculture in Colorado*, the "nine-days' wonder" in the western fruit regions never got beyond the promotion stage, and nothing more was heard of the seedless apple.

BEFORE THE WORMS ARRIVED

Delta's $100 Offer

In 1892, a Delta newspaper offered $100 to anyone who could bring in a wormy apple. The prize was never claimed. The apple worms arrived several years later, transported into the area by the railroads.

THE BIG APPLE

Chiles' Monster

In 1898, a huge apple was exhibited at the Delta County Fair in Delta. It became known as the "Paonia Apple" and was the Black River variety. Believed to set a national record, it measured twenty-seven inches in circumference, nine inches in diameter, and weighed thirty-four and three quarter ounces. The apple was grown by George P. Chiles of Paonia, who had an oil painting made of the prize fruit before he sold it for a dollar. Other gigantic apples from the same tree sold for twenty-five cents each.

WHEN PRESIDENT TAFT CAME TO
THE PEACH FESTIVAL

Locals Angled for the High Line Canal

President William Howard Taft was a hefty man, weighing in at 325 pounds. He had an infectious smile and a great sense of humor. From September through November of 1909, he went on a grand tour of the West, his special train equipped with a huge bathtub.

On his way to dedicate the Gunnison River diversion tunnel out of the Black Canyon at Montrose, he made a visit to Grand Junction. There, on September 22, he was welcomed to the Peach Festival at the County Fairgrounds (now Lincoln Park) where more than 8,000 people reportedly showed up for the first Presidential visit to the Grand Valley.

Taft praised the wonders of irrigation and was told what a High Line Canal north of the river would do to increase the agriculture of the valley. He was given a bushel of peaches by the Peach Queen Agnes Swisher of Palisade, and then rushed off to Montrose after saying he would support the High Line Canal project. Eventually, the canal was opened in 1917. The rotary dam in DeBeque Canyon was built by a German company and was delayed by World War I. Since the Germans lost the war, they were never fully paid for the contract.

FED UP WITH THE FEDS

"New Dealing" with Loma Farmers

Franklin D. Roosevelt's "New Deal" programs during the Depression years of the 1930s probably prevented more drastic revolutionary movements. But they also created more bureaucracy than the nation had ever experienced, and many of federal agents were unprepared to carry out their duties.

Recent college graduates were employed to deal with agricultural reform, which included cutting down on production to maintain prices at a time when there was very little cash in consumer pockets, and even less available to farmers and ranchers. Some of these agents showed up to visit Mesa County farms, even though few of them knew anything about farming.

Gertrude Rader and her husband farmed near the town of Loma, and she remembered, many years later, the frustrations encountered during those visits by the Mesa County Oral History Project. She recalled the time when agents shot one calf and two hogs to limit their livestock holdings. They did later receive a check in the amount of seven dollars for their "critters." The Raders were ordered to bury the dead animals, but after the agents left, the carcasses were dug up and made into corned beef and salt pork. Then the jars of meat were stored in the fruit cellar behind canned vegetables. Thus they had done as they promised: "We buried all that meat, though it was under the vegetables."

One agent figured the compensation for plowing under a field by stepping off a plot of land. Since his steps were more than three feet apart, the farmer got an exaggerated settlement. Another official could not distinguish oats from alfalfa seed.

When the Fruita Civilian Conservation Corps (CCC) showed up to poison prairie dogs, they placed poisoned oats around each hole in the Raders' cow pasture. One cow died from eating the oats, and others became very sick. No compensation was given when a complaint was made.

Since figuring irrigation water allotments was a science unknown to an agent from the East, Mrs. Rader, Secretary-Treasurer of the Loma Ditch and Lateral Association, spent two hours figuring out water requirements for him. He admitted anger and embarrassment at having a woman show him how to do the figuring. She said the contempt in the word "woman" caused her to throw all her figures in the fire and leave him to refigure for himself. In spite of all this, Mrs. Rader did have a few good words for the New Deal resettlement programs and even the CCC.

THE PRESIDENT AND THE PEACH

When Dewey Was Sure to Win

At least three U.S. Presidents have given talks in Grand Junction. William Howard Taft stopped here in 1912 on his way to open the Gunnison River diversion tunnel in Montrose, giving a talk at the Peach Festival. Gerald Ford gave a campaign speech at Lincoln Park. Harry Truman gave two whistle-stop talks from the Presidential railroad train.

The first of Truman's visits was in September of 1948, when his campaign for a second term seemed doomed. Pollster Elmo Roper had stopped recording national attitudes because challenger Thomas Dewey was so far in the lead that the election was "in the bag" and almost all political commentators agreed. Still thinking he could win, Truman set off on a thirty-three day tour of 21,929 miles, zigzagging through most states and stopping at as many as sixteen towns and cities a day.

It is well known that President Truman was a history buff and had a staff of four men working in Washington to research the history, economics, and politics of every town where the train would stop. When he appeared in Grand Junction on September 21, 1948, people were pleased that he knew of the origins of the city, its pioneer struggles, and the irrigation which had made the Grand Valley famous for its agriculture, especially in peach production. He commented:

> *Colorado, you know, is about half made up of Missourians. Every place I go, when people came in to see me, they very carefully informed me that they themselves were born in Missouri, or that their parents came from Missouri to Colorado. It was a long time, you know, before the people east of the Mississippi River could understand that the people out here don't wear horns and a tail. Some of them still think that.*

Truman's wife, Bess, and daughter, Margaret, appeared with him near the end of his short talk. Someone presented a basket of peaches to him, and when he tasted the fruit, he said it was the best peach he'd ever tasted. Before the train left to go to Utah, it was loaded with bushels of peaches for the reporters, staff, secret service men, and the train crew. That led to his comment to reporters, "I'll be eating peaches all the way to Washington," a quote that was picked up by the national press and radio commentator broadcasts.

It may have been such remarks that led to perhaps the greatest upset of any election in U.S. history when Truman was elected in November. Colorado was one of the states he won. He made another whistle-stop talk in 1952, campaigning for Democratic presidential candidate Adlai Stevenson. If he remembered the peach, there was no comment recorded.

BUSY BEES

Twenty-Two Tons of Honey

In late March 1928, the Grand Junction Fruit Grower's Association shipped an entire carload of honey to New York. There were 1,830 cases of honey, weighing twenty-two tons.

Many years later, Palisade's meadery was the first place in Colorado to produce mead, a honey wine. The term "meadery" is not in the dictionary. It was copyrighted by Fred and Connie Strothman for their unique winery.

COLORADO'S FIRST
BEET SUGAR FACTORY

*Financed With Riches
from Mining Camps*

Who first established the idea of making sugar from beets in Grand Junction?

Charles Boetcher was an immigrant from Germany who ran a hardware business in Leadville, supplying the silver boom with equipment to pull riches from the mountains. By the 1890s, Boetcher was a millionaire living in Denver. On a trip to his native Germany, where sugar beets were grown, he realized the soil and climate in the Grand Valley would be ideal to produce sugar beets. In 1897, he returned with a bag of seeds and started the growing of

In 1899 the first sugar beet factory in Colorado opened in Grand Junction.

Frank Dean photo, Loyd Files Research Library,
Museum of Western Colorado, 1982.101.

beets. Henry Rhone and Peter Magees of Grand Junction were pioneer growers along with other wealthy Denverites who founded the Colorado Sugar Manufacturing Company.

One of the partners was John F. Campion, who had made millions of dollars from silver and later gold mining in the Leadville district. He shared ownership of the Little Jonny Mine with J.J. Brown, said to be its discoverer. Brown has been most famous as "Leadville Johnny," estranged husband of the famous "Unsinkable" Molly Brown. Campion's biographers credit Campion as the organizer and founder of the sugar company. Another partner was J.R. McKinnie, who had reaped a fortune mining in the San Juan Mountains and at Cripple Creek, Colorado.

An annual total of 30,000 tons of beets were produced, and the average grower netted thirty dollars an acre — better than other crops. A $350,000 sugar beet factory opened in December of 1899, operated at full production during a six-week harvest campaign, and employed fifty men on each of two twelve-hour shifts. A second factory was established at Delta.

Boetcher was later instrumental in founding the Great Western Sugar Company and its many factories in the West. Then his corporation became the leading financial investment firm in Denver. Today, the Boetcher Foundation engages in many philanthropic programs, including college scholarships to outstanding Colorado high school students.

After World War II, the Climax Molybdenum Company purchased the local sugar beet plant and new equipment was brought in to process uranium. After the market for uranium declined, the buildings and radioactive tailings piles had to be removed to a desert disposal spot, and the land was converted into pleasant, non-hazardous parks.

BIOLOGICAL WARFARE

The Palisade Bug House

When Al Merlino was discharged from the Navy in 1946, he returned to Palisade to a job in the newly opened Colorado Insectary. After working there for thirty-eight years, he probably became one of the most knowledgeable entomologists in the nation.

After an oriental fruit moth was spotted in the railroad yards at Grand Junction in 1944, the Board of Control of the Mesa County Peach Marketing Order and the Colorado Department of Agriculture joined forces to combat that devastating insect.

By 1945, the Colorado Insectary was raising so-called "Mac" parasites to attack the moths, which invaded orchards the next year. A decade later, the laboratories released over eight million of the Macs and engaged in international cooperation to fight other harmful insects.

DDT had been widely used during and after World War II. Not only did it have a deadly effect on the ecological chain, but it also led to the evolution of "super" insects that were resistant to the

Paonia Insectary — "Bug House."

poison. When Rachel Carson's famous book, *Silent Spring*, was published in 1962, the public outcry against DDT led to its elimination in the United States as an insect controller. Popularly known as the "Palisade Bug House," the insectary has become instrumental in the development of biological control of pests. It is also involved in biological weed control through the use of insects.

Sign at Lyle Nichols' Sculpture Garden East Orchard Mesa. Further down the road, Carlson Vineyards placed a nude manaquin in the grapevines, startling some tourists.

Cattle, Sheep, and Horses

EXTENDING A LOAN

They Say it Really Happened

The best-known story about Fred Starr was set during the early 1920s, when he ran sheep on Piñon Mesa. It seems he was far behind on payments due on a mortgage against his sheep herd. There was so little hope for a further extension on his huge flock that he brought his sheep down to either be sold or shipped. The bank holding the loan was located on Main Street in Grand Junction and had threatened foreclosure.

Fred went into the bank and told the president that he simply had to have an extension. The president answered, "I'm sorry Fred. It's either the money or the sheep!"

"OK," Starr answered. He went to the bank's door and waved his hand. The president looked out and saw 4,000 sheep headed down Main Street toward the bank.

The bank president extended the loan.

WHY THE HORSES WENT WILD

And the Free Spirit of Dapple King

Technology and economic climate had much to do with the release of many domesticated horses in the early Twentieth Century. As tractors, trucks, and automobiles replaced the need for horses, they were no longer essential for transportation and farming. When beef production in western Colorado was increased, grassland became too precious to share with horses.

Wild Horse Statue DeBeque.

Then came the economic depression of the 1930s, and owning horses was an expensive luxury for ranchers and farmers. Many horses were shot; others just strayed into the non-productive and inaccessible Bookcliffs, in the canyons and ridges of northern Mesa County.

Finally, a movement was started to round up the wild horses and offer them for adoption. Others were assigned protected areas — one of which was the Little Book Cliffs

49

Wild Horse Area. Established in 1974, it occupies over 36,000 acres and can be entered from DeBeque and Cameo.

David L. Wheeler has studied that region and related the story of "Dapple King," an independent-minded stallion. Dapple King would always escape the roundups aimed to drive horses into protected area. From 1975 until 1983, he kept escaping the drivers. Finally, using a helicopter and radio transmitter, six horseback riders were able to drive Dapple King into a trap after a seven-mile, two-hour run.

While other horses were sent up for adoption, the wild free spirit of this one stallion was so admired that his captors released him, and he was never seen again.

THE GREAT WHITEWATER
WILD HORSE ROUNDUP

They Were Headed for South Africa

During the Boer War, 1899-1902, the British were running short of horses in their struggle against the Dutch for control of South Africa. Late in 1899, a British cavalry officer arrived at Whitewater, then a thriving town and a stopover on the long journey between Delta and Grand Junction.

The military man offered a dollar for every wild horse that could be captured and broken enough to be loaded into railroad cars bound for ships going to South Africa. More than four hundred horses were captured for the long journey. Historian Muriel Marshall wrote that one cowboy, Ralph Stoner, supplied most of the animals. Stoner reaped a very impressive amount of money for his part of the deal.

During World War I, Whitewater was again a shipping point for military horses that had been raised on ranches and sold to the United States Army. Some of the horses ended up in the battlefields of France during that war.

ABOUT THE BASQUES AND
THEIR BALL COURT

Remembering Urruty and Elizondo

While the unique Basque culture in western America is well known in Nevada, Idaho, and California, they also played an important role — mainly as sheepherders — in Mesa County and northwest Colorado. The ball court at Canyon View Park in Grand Junction is a monument to the Basque heritage.

Basques come from the Pyrenees Mountains, which form the border between France and Spain. They are neither French nor Spanish, having their own language and customs for at least two millennia. Two of the most famous saints of the Roman Catholic Church, Ignatius of Loyola and Francis Xavier, were Basques. Loyola founded the Jesuit Order, and Xavier was a famous missionary to China, Japan, and the East Indies. He established Christianity in Japan at Nagasaki.

Antonio Retolazi and his uncle, Antonio Coscorroso, bought a boarding house at 224 Colorado Avenue in Grand Junction from a former sheepherder, José Ocamica. After buying his uncle's share, it became the Retolazi Boarding House and Pool Hall and served three meals a day. Grand Junction became the center of Basque culture in western Colorado and eastern Utah. The boarding house was sold in 1947.

In 1935, Jean Urruty bought the LaSalle Hotel in Grand Junction at Second Street and Colorado Avenue and ran it for twenty years. Born in the Pyrenees, he became a successful sheep rancher in the Grand Valley and married Benerita Dolores Vasquez. The hotel welcomed Basques as well as any other transients, but had one absolute rule: no member of the Ku Klux Klan would be welcome. The Urrutys lived at 24th and C Road and hosted the Twelfth Annual Basque Festival there in 1972. In April of 1978, Jean built the ball court. It is believed that the court was intended for jai alai, a fast

Basque Ball Court.

and sometimes deadly game invented by the Basques. It involved using a curved basket, or "cesta," to throw a hard ball, or "pelota," against the wall at almost unbelievable speeds, where it would careen back possibly causing serious injury to the player. Today, it is mainly used as a ball court.

Urruty was noted for his many contributions to Basque culture and, in 1977, was given a generosity award by the American Basque Association. He helped make two television documentaries for *National Geographic* magazine. He died in 1983 at the age of eighty-one. The Urruty land was eventually purchased for Canyon View Park, but the ball court had long been available to anyone, according to Jean, "except the Ku Klux Klan." Plans to tear down the landmark court were met with so much public protest that it remains as a monument to Basque culture in the Grand Valley.

Perhaps the most successful sheep rancher in this region was Emmett Elizondo, who eventually made his home in Grand Junction. Born in the Spanish Basque country in 1897, he came to

GRAND MESA

COUNTRY

53

America on a ship dodging German submarines in 1917, during World War I. His first employment was as a sheepherder near Buffalo, Wyoming. With several partners, he purchased sheep and land, which grew into many thousands of acres in Utah, Colorado, Wyoming, and even Kansas. His summer range was north of the Black Canyon National Park.

When he was over fifty years of age, he returned to his homeland and fell in love with a nurse, Maria, whom he invited to Colorado. When she arrived, they were married and had a son, Jay, who became a design engineer for the International Harvester Corporation. Emmett eventually owned the vast Warren Ranch near Cheyenne, one of Wyoming's largest and most famous ranches. Chris Jouflas of Grand Junction, president of the American Sheep Producers Council, praised Emmett for his generosity to various organizations, as well as his management of sheep grazing lands.

Of course, all was not pleasant in his career. Emmett was a victim of the cattle and sheep wars of the 1920s, but eventually was successful in gaining the respect of cattlemen when they realized they could profitably raise both cattle and sheep. Emmett died in 1992 and Maria died in 1999. Both graves are in the Orchard Mesa Cemetery.

RAISING THOROUGHBRED
RACE HORSES

Dan Casement's Outfit and Tom "Silent" Smith

In the early Colorado land settlements of 1882, General John Stephen Casement founded a ranch near the Unaweep Canyon Divide. His son, Dan, who graduated from Princeton University in 1891, re-named it the "Triangle Bar Ranch." Dan and a friend, Tot Otis, had cultivated a taste for race horses and joined forces to buy and breed thoroughbreds. In 1910, Dan purchased a horse named Concho Coconell, sire of several famed racers. The most famous of these was Ballymooney, born on the ranch in 1914, and a nationally known winner. Ballymooney himself sired six notable racers by eight different mares.

From 1916-1921, the trainer at the ranch was Tom "Silent" Smith, who lived in Grand Junction. His ability to work with horses became nationally known when he trained the champion Seabiscuit in the 1930s. Smith died in 1957. Interest in him was revived due to Laura Hilenbrand's spellbinding book *Seabiscuit*. The story was filmed with Chris Cooper playing Smith's part.

Casement Ranch, Unaweep Canyon.

COWBOY PHILOSOPHER

The Remarkable Don Meek

George Stewart, whose father was founder of the Stewart Ditch near Paonia, spent much of his childhood on the family ranch on Minnesota Creek. In later life, he wrote his autobiography, *The Sowing and the Reaping*, in which he introduced Don Meek, one of the most gifted cowmen ever to ride in the North Fork country.

Don was at one time foreman of the Stewart Ranch. He also had a small ranch of his own near Black Canyon National Park. Stewart called Don "a natural philosopher of singular intellectual gifts." Meek was an avid reader and given to the art of thinking about the reasons for existence.

Don had a rich background, having "ridden the rods" as a hobo all over the United States and worked as a cowpoke, miner, hunter, and even a carpenter. He was considered a wizard with anything to do with cows and horses. As a sportsman, he competed in wrestling matches and was a crack shot with a rifle.

What was even more unusual about Don Meek was his ability to provoke thought, especially in the youngsters with whom he often rode or camped. Stewart called him an "original thinker and a creative listener." Don taught logic, ethics, and theological problems in simple terms, allowing his listeners to expand their knowledge.

Meek was not given to the obscene or prurient language common with many cowhands. He never promoted any particular religious theology, but encouraged thought about the nature of God. He held land, water, animals, and men as sacred, and he struck Stewart as something of a pantheist.

When discussing controversial ideas in politics or moral behavior, Meek would present more than one conflicting view, leaving it to others to struggle with the problems and resolve them individually. Actions of political leaders in Delta County were viewed in the same perspective. Why did the Commissioners make the decisions they did, and might there have been a better decision? Like Socrates, he asked questions but rarely gave answers.

Some time early in the Twentieth Century, Meek established a cattle ranch near Sapinero, on the southern side of the Black Canyon. He married a beautiful and gifted daughter of a British clergyman, and they raised two sons.

Town and

Road

Builders

STAKING OUT WEST DENVER

Sooners Jumped the Gun

Within three days of the Utes being expelled from their western Colorado territory to the Utah Reservation in September of 1881, a number of anxious settlers, or "sooners," showed up at the site of Grand Junction. Possibly the first two men to cross the Colorado River and stake claims were Douglas Baine and Art Hotchkiss. They followed what has come to be known as the North Branch of the Old Spanish Trail, waded the river, and put down stakes.

It was a surprise to them when they found another stake already in place, with the lettering "West Denver" on it. It was probably placed there by J.C. Nichols, William McGinley, and O.D. Russell, who had not waited for the opening of the Ute lands to grab a claim.

Baine built a tiny hut on the north bank of the river, using cottonwood logs. The following spring, he cleared a patch of land and seeded it with peach pits, which he said had to be cracked so they would come up that year. There is no evidence they did come up. Settlers on Rapid Creek above Palisade had better luck.

Only a few days after the "sooners" arrived, the Crawford Party established the town of Ute and then changed the name to "Grand Junction." The name "West Denver" never caught on.

A SICKLY MAN STAKED HIS CLAIMS

The Founder of Grand Junction and Delta

George A. Crawford may rightly be considered the founder of both Delta and Grand Junction. He also waged a life-long war with sickness and bodily weakness. Crawford was born in Pennsylvania in 1827. While in college there, he had to be sent home on account of ill health. Despite expectations that he would be too sick to work, he returned to his studies and embarked on a law career while publishing a newspaper. He never married.

In 1857, Crawford went to Kansas, then a hotbed of dissent between pro- and anti-slavery factions. The eastern portion of the state lent itself to good farming, and George founded the town of Fort Scott on the site of an abandoned military base. There he bought a sawmill, along with a pro-slavery hotel that he made into a free-state hotel.

When pro-slavery men formed a militant gang known as the "Bloody Reds," they sent Crawford a note: "You are respectfully invited to leave town in twenty-four hours." George commented, "I don't

George Crawford, president of Grand Junction Town Company.
Mesa County Public Library Collecion, Loyd Files Research Library, Museum of Western Colorado, 1979.116.

exchange messages with horse thieves." While the gang did not attack Crawford, they did kill eleven free state men. The incident became known as the "Marias des Cyones Massacre," later chronicled in a poem by Whittier.

In 1861, Crawford ran for governor of Kansas and attained a majority of the votes. The election was voided due to a constitutional violation, but from that time on he was called "Governor Crawford," even though he never served a day in that office. He did, however, found the Kansas Historical Society.

Still plagued with poor health, he went to Gunnison, Colorado, in 1881, and, with R.D. Mobley and M. Rush Warner, joined the land rush when the Utes were evacuated from western Colorado. They visited a site they called "Uncompahgre," after the Ute name for the river. The party continued down the Gunnison River to its confluence with the Grand River. On September 26, 1881, Crawford claimed the site as Grand Junction. Earlier arrivals had called the settlement "Ute" and even "West Denver," a term that would horrify some modern residents. The next week, he returned to establish Delta, a name adapted when people could not pronounce the word Uncompahgre. Crawford employed Samuel Wade, founder of the town of Paonia, to survey both community sites.

Tomb of the founder of Grand Junction.

Photo by Randy Fay

Among George's projects in Grand Junction was the building of its first hotel, a brick factory, and several houses. He established and published the *Grand Junction Daily Star*, the town's first newspaper. Later he developed local orchards and by 1889 could claim that 2,800 carloads of fruit were shipped from his trees, although that figure probably represented all of the valley orchards.

When "Governor" Crawford died of tuberculosis in 1891, he was entombed on the hill that overlooks the two rivers, just above the Orchard Mesa Cemetery. His *Daily Star* commented, "Many will mourn; many a tear will be shed o'er the grave of the brave little man whose life, filled as it was with adversity and affliction, yet became, through a magnificent will and genius, the most earnest and useful that we have ever known."

EXPLOITS OF THE AMAZING ENOS T.

Before He Founded Hotchkiss

Much has been written about Enos T. Hotchkiss and how he illegally entered the Ute reservation to make his permanent home in the area that now bears his name. He was a clever and stealthy man who managed to out-maneuver the Utes stalking his explorations. Enos also was a log rafter; flour mill builder; explorer and prospector; father of ten children by two wives; founder of Lake City, Colorado; road builder; farmer; and cattle and sheep rancher.

Born in Bradford Hill, Pennsylvania, in 1832, he was the second of six children. He was only nine years of age when his father died. Enos and two of his brothers established a log floating enterprise on the Allegheny River from Bradford to Pittsburgh, and at one time ran a log raft from Minnesota to Rock Island, Illinois.

When their mother re-married, the three eldest Hotchkiss brothers, Roswell, Enos, and Preston, set out for the West. Nebraska credits them with having constructed the first flour mill in that state, in 1857. Roswell remained in Nebraska while Enos and Preston went to the Dakota Territory, where they were involved with ranching and prospecting.

Enos had married fourteen-year-old Hannah Seeley in 1851, and they had a son, Andrew, and a daughter named Ida. When the Colorado gold rush hit, Enos headed to Denver, driving a wagon, and carrying little Andy on his shoulders. Denver at that time was little more than a conglomeration of hastily built shacks and tents. Enos built a cabin near present-day Morrison, Colorado, and worked odd jobs. Two more children were born there, Ellen and Charles.

Enos spent over five years prospecting the Rockies and is believed to have done the first scouting of the Ragged Mountain area, above Paonia. He also spent time prospecting in Nevada, Montana, and California and finally discovered that he could make

Enos T. Hotchkiss from the Northfork Times.

more money by growing grain to feed mules than in prospecting for gold. When Enos returned, he found that Hannah had borne a child by another man, claiming she thought Enos must have died. Enos divorced her, and she married the father of the new child.

In the years that followed, Enos lived in Del Norte and Saguache, which became the jumping-off points for prospectors in the San Juan Mountains. In Saguache, he went into a partnership with Otto Mears, the famed "Pathfinder of the San Juans," noted for his numerous roads and railroads in that region. In 1874, Mears gave him the contract to build a road over Cochetopa and Slumgullion passes.

One source relates that he was the first to find the remains of the companions of Alferd Packer, who, it was claimed, had murdered and cannibalized his partners during the previous winter. At nearby Lake San Cristobal, Enos discovered a lode, which became one of the greatest in Colorado history as a source of gold and silver. Long known as the Hotchkiss Mine, it was later named the Golden Fleece. He was able to borrow (and soon repay) $100,000 to develop the mine.

Hotchkiss built the first cabin in Lake City and then laid out the original town. A nearby mountain was named for him. In 1877, he returned to Denver, where he met and married a widow, Elizabeth Cowan, who had one son, Jake. They lived in Lake City until Enos fell into the shaft of his mine and was injured, lying for several days at the bottom of the mine before he was rescued.

After that, he sold the mine and took up ranching at Powderhorn, located between Lake City and Gunnison. It was from there, in 1881, that Enos entered the newly opened reservation lands to establish the town of Hotchkiss. With the proceeds from his ranch, he bought a flock of sheep, much to the chagrin of other ranchers; but after all, he was the famous Enos T. Hotchkiss, so they allowed for his whim.

Enos and Elizabeth had six children together: Fred, Addie, and Enos Clair were born at Powderhorn; Gertrude, Adair, and Leon were born at Hotchkiss. Enos died in 1900; Elizabeth four years later. They, their six children, and Elizabeth's son, Jake, were all interred in the Hotchkiss Cemetery. What a man he was! The National Cowboy Hall of Fame honored Hotchkiss' memory in 1961.

THERE IS ONLY ONE PAONIA

But Once There Was Another

Samuel Wade, the founder of Paonia, was a great admirer of the peony plant. He originally gave the town the name of Paeonia. In the Greek form, the "a" and "e" were combined into one letter, and that is how it appeared in biology books. Apparently, the postal service was going to have none of those weird letters around, and they shortened the name to Paonia. The peonies growing at the base of the miner's statue in the Paonia City Park are believed to be the direct descendants of the rootstock Wade planted in 1882.

Wade may have been a student of the classics and studied accounts of the ancient land of Paeonia found in the Iliad. The people of Paeonia were famous for their barley beer and the medicines they made from plants and herbs. One of the flowers was the paeonia, named for Paeon, the medical doctor for the Greek gods. When Persia's emperor, Darius the Great, invaded Greece, he saw a remarkable lady carrying a pitcher on her head, leading a horse to drink, and spinning flax, all at the same time. He was informed that she was a Paeonian. Believing that all the people of that country must be hard workers, he gave orders for two of their tribes to be sent to Persia to teach his people how to be more industrious.

The land of Paeonia was reported to be rich in gold, and there were stories of a bituminous kind of wood that would burst into flame when it made contact with water!

While there were a number of independent tribes in this land, which was described as beautiful and lush, they were ruled by one king. Homer reputed their men to be very good soldiers. In spite of that, the land was overrun by Gallic invaders in 280 A.D. and was absorbed into the also-conquered country of Macedonia.

There is only one Paonia left in the world, and, by Greek tradition, it should be known for hard-working women, brave men, and great medicinal powers.

GETTING CLEAN WATER TO FRUITA

Twenty-Three Miles of Wooden Pipes

One of the dreadful problems with using the water taken from rivers was that of disease — especially typhoid fever. An outbreak in the mining country above Ouray would mean that within a day Montrose would be hit, then Delta, Grand Junction, and Fruita.

By 1897, some Colorado towns had been able to get water from wells and other sources, but Fruita concluded that it must have pure water from the mountains. The town bought land and built several dams on Piñon Mesa above Glade Park.

Then came one of the most challenging engineering projects in the history of Mesa County. Forty to fifty carloads of wooden pipe were brought to the town during the winter. Since the Colorado River could only be crossed by ferry, except in winter when there was no service, the wooden pipes had to be transported via a cage that was connected to a cable strung across the river. Two men were killed in accidents involving that operation.

After that was the overwhelming job of getting the pipes on a good drainage pattern over cliffs, along narrow ledges, and around monoliths, much of it on what would become Colorado National Monument. In 1907, after a decade of digging and blasting, Fruita completed the twenty-three mile-long pipeline. It then had the first mountain water supply in the valley. The project was funded through a $130,000 bond issue.

Federal officials moved the line and installed steel pipes in return for a ten-percent water allotment for the Colorado National Monument in 1935. Only during the following year did the spring-fed reservoirs dry up and force Fruita to boil river water again. While the lakes still exist, the town no longer uses the line, getting its supply from the Ute Water District.

MR. RHONE'S ROAN CREEK ROAD

It Went Through Hogback Canyon

Henry Rhone was one of the first citizens to settle in Grand Junction and had a great vision to connect the city to towns to the east. He worked as an attorney, a real estate and mining promoter, and also served as mayor.

At that time, Grand Junction was isolated from Parachute, Rifle, and Glenwood Springs because of the narrow "Hogback Canyon," now called "DeBeque Canyon" of the Colorado River. Travelers coming from that direction would have to turn up Roan Creek, follow the north side of the Bookcliff Mountains west to Salt Wash near Fruita, and then descend into the Grand Valley. Historian Donald MacKendrick estimated that on that route it took one hundred miles to reach Grand Junction, only thirty-five miles away.

Another route would lead up to the Plateau Valley, over the formidable Hogback to Rapid Creek and what became Palisade, an effort which sometimes required unhitching wagons and lowering them down the steep grades.

It became apparent to Rhone that a toll road through the canyon was necessary. After many failed attempts to raise the estimated $100,000 needed for the project, he was able to complete the road for only $12,500. The route followed the north side of the river from a point west of Palisade to the Roan Creek confluence at the east end of the canyon, a distance of about twenty-five miles. There it connected with established roads to the east.

Among the road investors was W.T. Carpenter, whose coal-mining town north of Grand Junction was the terminus of his fabled Little Bookcliff Railroad. Tolls for use of the road ranged from three dollars for a team and wagon, to loose livestock at 22.5 cents each. Regular stagecoach service and freight lines were established.

In 1889, the Denver and Rio Grande Railway purchased the route and by 1890 completed laying its tracks to Grand Junction. Once again, wagons would have to use the then-improved Hogback and Rapid Creek route until the Plateau Creek Road was constructed in the next century.

OTTO'S INTERSTATE HIGHWAY?

That Delightful Trail of the Serpents

One of the most popular hikes in Colorado National Monument is the zig-zag Serpent's Trail near the east entrance to the Monument. It was not always just a trail, being at one time hailed by John Otto, the man who built it, as part of what he planned would be an Interstate Highway crossing the nation!

Lila M. Wills, former Fruita librarian, wrote a meticulous history of that trail, named *Tale of the Serpent*. In it, the author traced the vision of John Otto, who, in 1913, started work on the trail with volunteers. Carved on the steep formation on the west side of No Thoroughfare Canyon, the trail rises over 1,000 vertical feet, taking two and one quarter miles, with fifty switchbacks, to reach the top of the massive cliff. By 1915, it was open for pedestrians and horseback riders.

When the automobile came of age, Otto developed an even more ambitious plan. At that time, the so-called Midland autoroute across the nation included a long desert stretch between Mack, Colorado, and Cisco, Utah. That route had no sources of water and became a quagmire when even moderate rains swept the area. Otto proposed his trail be turned into a road going to Glade Park and then to the Utah border and on to Cisco. That route would require only one interruption, a ferry ride across the Colorado River. It would then join a road already coming to Cisco from the west, and thus complete the "interstate" highway. He noted that the region traversed would be much more stable than the desert, and it had much more appealing scenery.

At that time, the only existing route to Glade Park from Grand Junction was what is known now as the Little Park Road, a distance of twenty miles. John Otto's proposal would cut the mileage to only eleven and one-half miles, and would be on more stable terrain.

Thus the Glade Park ranchers and farmers pledged $4,000 to widen the Serpent's Trail, Mesa County contributed $12,000, and other donations totaled $3,000.

By 1917, the road was complete to the top of Piñon Mesa. It was nineteen feet wide, to permit the passing of two vehicles. Later, it was extended to Glade Park and would eventually connect with another of Otto's dreams, the rimrock road along the entire length of the Monument.

Mesa County bought the property leading to the trail, and then the federal government greatly enlarged the Colorado National Monument to include a substantial part of the No Thoroughfare Canyon, including the "highway."

The Civilian Conservation Corps and other workers constructed Rimrock Drive in the 1930s. By then, Otto had been fired as superintendent of the Monument, and there was no further talk of an interstate highway. The Serpent's Trail road served until 1950, when the government built the current alternate route, including tunnels, to the top. In 1959, Mesa County vacated its claim to the road, and years later, the Monument re-opened it as a trail.

In addition to many trails on the Monument, Otto developed two trails above Palisade and Clifton, traversing the sides of Mount Garfield and Mount Lincoln. To those, he added the trail now known as the Land's End Road on the west side of Grand Mesa. He proposed that it too should become part of the "interstate" and that Grand Mesa be designated, along with Colorado National Monument, as a national park.

A TOWN CALLED WELCOME

On the Delta County Redlands

If you have an envelope postmarked "Welcome, Colorado," it is quite rare, because that post office only survived for two years, from June of 1910 until August of 1912. Welcome was located just north of Lawhead Gulch on the Redlands in Delta County at a spot later occupied by the Wigger farm, then called 2636 N Road. Nearby was the West Redlands School, often referred to as the Welcome School. There was also a community church and a small store inside the post office building which stocked a few staples.

It served as a center for quite a few families in the area, drawn together by the church and school. No one seems to know why the name "Welcome" was chosen. Seventy years later, Redlands resident John R. Mihelich did a study of the post office and some of the happenings at Welcome during its short life. The town was very active, with a Republican Party rally at the schoolhouse and various holiday celebrations. The missionary ladies of the church collected and repaired old clothing for poor children at Pueblo. Mrs. C.D. Seeley entertained fourteen bachelors for Christmas dinner in 1910. A hayrack ride turned nearly upside-down, with the revelers not returning until 4:30 A.M.

In those days, literary and debate societies were quite active as a form of community entertainment. The Welcome Literary Club was no exception, traveling as far as Eckert and Cedaredge for competitions, which brought remarkably large audiences to debates on U.S. foreign policy and the virtues or hazards of socialism. At the Welcome School on November 25, 1910, there was a great debate as to whether fire or water was most destructive. The "fire side" won.

One of the biggest events in western Colorado was the 1911 visit of President Taft for the dedication of the Gunnison Diversion

Tunnel in Montrose, and a large contingent of Welcome residents went to see him. However, within a short time, the government decided that the Hotchkiss post office was adequate to handle the mail for that area, and Welcome disappeared from the maps.

THAT MYSTERIOUS GRAVE ON THE LAND'S END ROAD

Who Was Buried There?

When the spectacular Land's End Road was completed in 1933, it was noticed that along the side of the road, there appeared to be a mound surrounded by rocks. It had a crude cross at one end, usually decorated with wildflowers. Laborers from the Works Progress Administration (WPA) had taken over the maintenance and improvement to the road, and several were asked about the mound, which was apparently a human grave.

There had been no report of deaths from the Civilian Conservation Corps (CCC) which had built the road, but it was assumed that the grave was that of a CCC worker. Several theories of the death circulated, and one version had the victim being shot by an Indian with a poisoned arrow. Still another claimed that two CCC boys had a fight in which one man split the other's head open.

Eventually there were demands that the body be exhumed and given a proper burial in Grand Junction. When the County Sheriff went to investigate the grave, he apparently learned the truth: during the repair of the road, one of the tractor operators built up a mound which looked like a six-foot grave. The WPA crew placed rocks around it as a joke, and then made a cross to stand at one end. Later, they began to supply flowers to expand upon the practical joke.

Over time, the "grave" was overgrown and neglected, and gradually forgotten. It was not until the 1980s that Nathan Robb, a worker on the road, told the true story of the "burial site" — nothing but road dirt.

Politics

and

Development

GRAND JUNCTION'S FLIRTATION WITH SOCIALISM

Was "Nature City" a "Hobo Haven?"

James W. Bucklin arrived in Grand Junction early in 1882, establishing a legal practice and working with founder George Crawford in planning the town. He soon found himself at odds with Crawford, an experienced town founder. Bucklin saw the new community as a virtual "Utopia," unique in governmental aims. Some called him a Socialist, but he considered himself "a pioneer in thought."

In 1884, Bucklin was elected to the Colorado House of Representatives as a Republican. In 1896, he was again elected to the House, this time as a Populist. In 1898, he went to the State Senate on a Populist-Democrat ticket. During these years, he was credited with getting the federal government to locate the Indian School in Grand Junction, and pushing the state to build a bridge over the Colorado River.

After the turn of the century, Bucklin was elected as city attorney and was later accused by Walter Walker, publisher of the *Daily Sentinel,* of being a Socialist "Boss" of the town. By 1909, Bucklin was an avowed Socialist and decided on a "clean-up" of his Utopia. The area south of downtown was notorious for its saloons and houses of prostitution. In the election of 1909, the citizens voted prohibition in, closing the saloons. The next year police began arresting prostitutes. In that same election, voters approved a new charter, calling for a "preferential ballot." Voters would mark first, second, and third choices of candidates. In this way, Socialist Thomas Todd was elected mayor, not because of a majority of first choices, but a majority of second and third choices.

Grand Junction has always been attractive to homeless people, probably because of its mild climate. The new government decided that hobos and unemployed men could chop wood in return for groceries from the city. Coal mine operators complained that the city was competing with private enterprise. A California newspaper claimed Grand Junction was a sort of hobo heaven where drifters could get three square meals a day at public expense.

Mayor Todd advocated that the city take over and operate the electric power system. In a campaign against "Bucklinism," publisher Walker persuaded voters to reject the electric system. During Todd's tenure, weeds and trash disposal were brought under control, and Main Street was paved. Todd was mentioned as a possible Socialist candidate for president.

In 1914, Bucklin paid for the publication of a pamphlet called *Nature City, The Ideal Commonwealth*. His description left no doubt that "Nature City" was Grand Junction and the ideals presented were a single land tax, municipal ownership of utilities, free trade, and other reforms. Although Socialism had been somewhat stifled by 1917, there were mass meetings of people opposed to the U.S. entry into World War I, claiming that only two percent of Grand Junction residents supported the war. Publisher Walker disagreed and claimed anyone opposed to war was unpatriotic.

Bucklin became ill in 1915 and retired to a California sanitarium where he died in 1919. His remains were returned to his "Utopia" for a funeral and burial.

A SURVIVING STRUCTURE

DeBeque's Odd Fellow's Hall

The distinctive pressed-metal building façades manufactured by Mesker Brothers of St. Louis, Missouri, and Evansville, Indiana, were once relatively common in western towns, but there are only a few of them left today. The advantages of the metal were low price, easy mounting on almost any framework, a slight degree of fireproofing, low maintenance costs, and a touch of the then fashionable Greek architecture. The material was usually thin steel that was coated with zinc, which could be painted to suit the builder.

One of the few remaining such façades in Colorado is located at the town of DeBeque. Today, the building is not used, but it still dominates the downtown section of that community. People used to call these edifices "tin buildings," and the DeBeque structure is now on the register of historic buildings in Colorado.

Built as a lodge hall for the Independent Order of Odd Fellows in 1903, it included a ballroom on the first floor, with ritual meeting rooms upstairs. All four sides of the structure

I.O.O.F. "Tin Building" DeBeque.

were covered with the pressed metal, shaped to look like stone blocks. The façade sports elaborate designs, including modified Doric columns, decorative finials on the top corners, and the top ledge engraved by the lodge initials, I.O.O.F..

While I.O.O.F. Lodge No. 125, "Roan Creek," was later absorbed by another branch, the old hall was used through the years for plays, movies, weddings, funerals, and dances, for which Armand DeBeque's dance band often performed.

To locate this landmark, just look for the largest structure in town, located at Fourth Street and Curtis Avenue. It has been preserved from rust corrosion by a cover of paint.

WHEN THE KLAN BURNED A
HOTCHKISS CHURCH

"All-American" Ideals

Following World War I, there was a revival of the infamous Ku Klux Klan, a secret terrorist society that had developed after the Civil War. At this time its main targets were blacks, Roman Catholics, and immigrants. By 1924, the hooded members had infiltrated the North Fork of the Gunnison towns and almost all of Colorado. A Denver dentist, Dr. John Galen Locke, ruled the "invisible empire" from a basement room in the capital city.

At that time there was no Catholic Church in Hotchkiss, but there was one in Lazear. In the spring of that year, the priest, Rev. Jeremiah O'Farrell, decided to move the church to Hotchkiss. O'Farrell was warned both by telephone and through indirect conversations that the church was not wanted in Hotchkiss.

Nevertheless, the church was established there with little harassment until one night in May 1924, when someone broke a window in the church, poured gasoline inside, and set it on fire. Local volunteer firemen were hampered in their efforts because all the nozzles had been removed from the hoses. In spite of that, they were able to extinguish the blaze before it burned down the church.

Repairs were made, and a reward of $500 was offered for the culprit or culprits responsible. Volunteers, including some non-Catholics, guarded the premises at night for several weeks, but no further attempts were made to destroy the building.

In July, a fiery cross, symbol of the Klan, was seen burning on Cedar Hill above Paonia. The Klan also ran a full-page advertisement in the local newspaper to explain their "all-American" ideals. The Klan managed to get member Clarence Morely elected Colorado governor, and Denver Mayor Ben Stapleton, although probably not a member himself, fell under control of the society, firing many Catholic and foreign-born employees of the city. By the time Morely's term expired in 1926, the people of Colorado had turned against the Klan, and it quickly dwindled in size.

WALKER'S SHORT STINT WITH THE KU KLUX KLAN

Later His Scathing Opposition

Walter Walker, publisher of Grand Junction's *Daily Sentinel* for four decades, certainly made some great contributions to the physical and cultural well-being of Mesa County. He was a great promoter of the Avalon Theater, Mesa Junior College, and the airport that was later named for him. He represented the Grand Junction area in the Colorado Assembly.

Walker was allegedly the second member of the Grand Junction Ku Klux Klan. During the post World War I days in Colorado, the Klan made a great impression by favoring prohibition and restriction of immigration. It championed reform and "100% Americanism." Dressed in hooded gowns, its secret membership paraded in cities and towns. The Klan feared and hated blacks, Hispanics, Irish, Italians, and any Roman Catholic immigrants.

In a clever manipulation, the Klan was able to infiltrate the Republican Party, and won the election of Clarence Morley as governor in 1924. For two years Klan politics ruled the state until the Republican Party disdained their own leader.

In Grand Junction, crosses were burned and great hooded parades were held. Walker was reported to have made vitriolic anti-Catholic speeches. Walker tried to gain control of the local Klan, expecting he would be given the title of Grand Kleagle. When another leader was chosen, Walker began a series of editorial attacks on the Klan, which caused his dismissal from membership "for violation of his obligation."

This led to a full exposure by the *Daily Sentinel* on the hooded order's activities. The newspaper ran a story headlined "The Bloody Toll of Incompetency," detailing Klan influence on the

Walter Walker, publisher of Grand Junction's Daily Sentinel, *1883-1956.*
Photograph courtesy of the *Daily Sentinel.*

police. It told of the killing of a Mexican bootlegger by the local officers and quoted a Klan member as saying the victim "was only a damned Mexican." A well-known business leader physically attacked Walker right on Main Street.

By 1926, the Republican Party had purged itself of Klan dominance, but it still lost the governance of Colorado to Democrat William H. "Billy" Adams, who had been endorsed by the *Daily Sentinel* as well as many other Colorado newspapers.

WHEN FRUITA CHANGED
A LAW OVERNIGHT

A Delicate Matter of Antiquated Racism

The prejudices of the Nineteenth Century were evident to the point that some towns in Colorado had written laws prohibiting blacks from staying in town overnight or being buried in local cemeteries.

But the bans were overlooked in the case of Charlie Glass, who died at age sixty-five in the early 1930s. His funeral and burial in the Fruita cemetery were very well attended. Charlie was a very popular black cowboy, ranch foreman, and rodeo performer. He had been acquitted in 1921 in the shooting of a Basque sheepherder, and, since at that time Basque sheepherders were often hated by cattlemen, the decision was widely supported.

In 1952, the Minters, a black family from Louisiana, had a car accident near Fruita, resulting in the death of one of the children. Fruita came to the aid of the victims, provided the family a house, gave a proper funeral for the child, and arranged care for the other children. Mr. Melvin Minter was even offered a job.

Then someone in Fruita remembered the old ordinance against blacks remaining in town after sundown. The local judge declined to enforce the law, and, as the law's violation could lead to further complications, he urged the city council to hold an emergency session to rescind the law. It passed unanimously. Mr. Minter expressed gratitude and praise to the council, pointing out that his family had never before been treated so well. The family settled in Fruita, and Mr. Minter once asked, "Why would a man leave a place like this?"

BIGGEST CITY IN DELTA COUNTY

Eleven Square Miles

The towns of Eckert and Corey have disappeared on many Colorado maps. In their place is a dot designated as Orchard City. Designed and incorporated as a single, clean water system in 1912, it had only that function. It also included the town of Austin. Orchard City includes eleven square miles, or 7,000 acres. Don't bother to look for its city hall or police department.

DEEP SEA DIVING IN A RESERVOIR

Solving a Plumbing Problem

In 1931, a newly laid fresh water pipe on the bed of the Fruitgrowers Reservoir in Hart's Basin east of Eckert broke, contaminating the pure drinking water. It became apparent that the only way to reach it was by using a deep-water diving suit. Such equipment is not generally available in the arid West, but, after much searching, a diving suit was found to be available for rent in Boston, Massachusetts. It was sent by express mail to Eckert within a week.

The next challenge arose when it was discovered that the suit was too small for the chosen repairman to wear, so a search began to find a smaller person who could be trained to do the repair job. After a suitable sized man was recruited, the inexperienced farmers on the boat had to be instructed on how to provide an air source for the diver, and also how to properly weight the diver so he would sink to the bottom. After many frustrated attempts, the break was found, and the leak was successfully repaired underwater.

A BUNGLED BANK ROBBERY

Waking Up DeBeque—Literally!

On May 9, 1913, $10,000 in cash had been placed secretly, supposedly, in the bank safe in DeBeque. However, two men attempted a break-in at 3 a.m. the next day, using dynamite to blow open the safe, and waking up the whole town.

A shoemaker, R.G. Harris, lived across from the bank and ran out the front door. He was ordered back into his house by the armed thugs who were planning another blast. Harris went out his back door and assembled the now-awakened citizens who grabbed their firearms. The culprits abandoned their efforts when "fire opened on them," but they somehow escaped penniless into the hills before a posse could be organized. An all-day search turned up no sign of the would-be robbers.

DeBeque Bank.

THE MANY LIVES OF
HANDY CHAPEL

Grand Junction's Oldest Church

In 1882, the Grand Junction Town and Improvement Company sold corners of blocks to church groups for only a dollar. One of the churches to take advantage of this was the African Methodist Episcopal Church, which had an all black membership, a very small minority of the earliest settlers.

The town had only existed a month when on October 9, 1882, the Reverend Isaac Witchel conducted the first formal church service in Grand Junction at the corner of Second Street and White Avenue. Some of the members were cowboys; others were staking claims to farming land. Two years later, many blacks were employed as miners at the coal mines at Carpenter, north of town, and were commuters on William Thomas Carpenter's Little Bookcliff (narrow-gauge) Railroad.

90   *Handy Chapel. Oldest Grand Junction church.*

By 1892, the parishioners had built a chapel on that site, and it is today the oldest church on its original site in Grand Junction. It was originally called Wright's Chapel for Silas Wright, the pastor. When a later pastor, William Handy, took over the church, it was called Handy Chapel, and that name has remained to this day.

The church has survived many crises, including declining membership. In the Ku Klux Klan days of the 1920s and the Depression years of the 1930s, there was widespread racism due to competition for jobs. Mexicans, Indians, Blacks, and Basques were banned from some restaurants and hotels. A Handy Chapel pastor, Brother Booker Thomas Washington Taylor, and his brother, Wesley, opened their homes to blacks traveling through or stranded in Grand Junction.

In 1979, declining membership prompted the Rocky Mountain Conference of the African Methodist Episcopal Church to sell the building and land to a group of local businessmen for $68,000. The local parish protested and won a court case declaring the sale illegal as the property belonged to the local congregation.

Handy Chapel became a non-denominational church, welcoming people of all races. A grant to restore the church to its original status led to its listing on the National Register of Historic Places in 1994. As of this writing, Handy Chapel has Saturday services for Seventh Day Adventists, Sunday morning services for the Independent True Vine congregations, and a Sunday afternoon service conducted in Spanish.

A MIRACLE ON MAIN STREET

The Unique Downtown Park

Grand Junction's downtown shopping mall has won many prizes and succeeded in keeping itself alive during a period in which many main streets in America have all but died. It was a prime factor in the 1963 award of "All-America City" to Grand Junction by the National Civic League, by *Look Magazine*, and George Gallop, the famous

Downtown Grand Junction Mall.

pollster. It was one of the earliest transformations in the U.S. of a downtown district into an attractive park.

How did this creative idea come to pass? As early as 1958, with the decline of the uranium boom, the economic prospects of Grand Junction were very gloomy. Then came the opening by Lloyd Files of the first shopping mall, Teller Arms on North Avenue, which included several major anchor stores. Some merchants and building owners were beginning to fear a retreat of business from the downtown area, which had remained essentially the same in the eighty years of Grand Junction history.

There were critical questions that arose from redesigning the street to a serpentine road and making a park with trees and flowers. Most critical was the presumed loss of parking space. Old water and sewer lines had to be replaced, and the massive construction undertaking was going to hurt business. Support from the city, financing from downtown business owners, and efforts of the Chamber of Commerce under the leadership of Dale Hollingsworth, all came together to make the dream a reality.

A committee appointed by the City Council and spearheaded by Joe Lacy, city manager, included Leland Schmidt, James Gormley, Barbara Hyde, Howard McMullen, Amos Ross, Rudolph Susonam, and architect Robert VanDusen.

Stores had to operate through their back doors during the reconstruction. By 1963, the main street shopping district had become what some have called the most beautiful downtown in Colorado! Later, the addition of the largest collection of outdoor sculpture in the state, "Art on the Corner," with both permanent and changing displays, made the park even more of an attraction. Since then, many malls and shopping centers have come to the Grand Junction area, but none can begin to match the beauty of Main Street.

THE RENAISSANCE OF DELTA

How to Become an "All-American" City

"Until recently, the city of Delta, Colorado, presented a picture of a small, rural city in decline. Old sewer lagoons, an abandoned sugar beet factory full of fine lime dust, and deteriorating streets and sidewalks testified to the decay." So read Delta's application for designation as an All-American City. A local businessman added, "There was low self-esteem, and all the communities around had a dislike of Delta. The air smelled, the dust blew, the streets were terrible."

The "recent time" was 1985, and, only seven years later, Delta won a national competition for the All-American City Award! What caused this great transformation? It's debatable, but one factor has to be attributed to the idea of eighty-one-year-old Gus Albert, a motel owner and a one-time Chamber of Commerce manager. He envisioned a pageant based on Delta's history. In the summer of 1986, the play Thunder Mountain Lives Tonight! was first performed by volunteers. It attracted many tourists, but probably more important was the excitement and pride it fostered among local area citizens. The pageant was performed five nights a week for the next ten summers, a total of 496, and the longest-running outdoor show in Colorado history. More than 160 volunteers took part in the productions.

Before long, other ideas took form in the minds of the Deltans. Work was begun to create Confluence Park on the grounds of the abandoned sugar beet factory. The park has a sixty-acre fishing lake, a wetlands nesting area that attracts bird watchers, and five miles of trails for walking, jogging, and biking. An amphitheater was built for the pageant and other events. Antoine Robidoux's Fort Uncompahgre dating from 1826 was faithfully restored and soon became a unique attraction of western Colorado tourism. Horse lovers developed an arena for equine performances.

Another dream began to materialize as funding was sought for a multi-million dollar recreation center, complete with a swimming pool, exercise rooms, and various meeting areas. When the Kuwait ambassador to the United States visited the town, he was so impressed that he pledged one hundred thousand dollars to the project in appreciation of the rescue of Kuwait in the Gulf War. He also pledged another five thousand dollars for Pioneer Town, a living history museum at nearby Cedaredge.

Businesses were soon attracted to the vicinity of Confluence Park. By 1992, there were two major retail stores, two restaurants, and a feed mill centered on the storage silos of the former sugar factory. Altogether seventy new jobs were created.

Delta's downtown was transformed with trees, flowers, and new storefronts. The community became a "City of Murals" when professional artists painted what have since become more than a dozen huge displays depicting Native Americans, Hispanic heritage, fruit-growing, and other farming and ranching endeavors, as well as other historic events in Delta history.

Mural Downtown Delta.

GRAND MESA COUNTRY

The elaborate art deco Egyptian movie theater was restored to its glory of the 1930s and designated as an historical preservation site. A new museum by the Delta County Historical Society was opened to display artifacts and promote local history. While there have been many hundreds of volunteers involved in all these projects, the imaginative city manager Steve Schutt has been acknowledged as the guiding force throughout the awakening.

Delta County schools, under Superintendent Laddie Livingston, developed the nation's initial learning program for students using computers to solve problems. It attracted visiting educators from all over America and foreign nations. The program became a model for what is now an almost universal practice in American schools. Delta County students were also winning state academic championships.

Thus, in 1992, Delta, with a population of 3,800, became the smallest town to win the All-American City Award. It is noteworthy that this was the second city in Thunder Mountain Country to attain that honor as Grand Junction had been so designated three decades earlier.

A TALE OF ZOO CITIES

Wildlife in Delta and Grand Junction

Dr. W.S. Cleland and the Federated Women's Club of Delta gave the city a park in 1921. Clarence Riley was hired to be the caretaker and, according to long-time civic leader Gordon Hodgins, "never changed jobs again." A drastic change in Riley's duties came in 1927 when a lady gave the park a peacock to accompany the beautiful gardens. A cage was built, and at dawn each day the peacock would scream "Help! Help! Help!" in what sounded like a human voice.

Neighbors became used to the alarming calls, and the Delta Lions Club decided that the peacock needed company. Before long, people donated a wolf, deer, mountain lion, monkeys, squirrels, pheasants, quail, red fox, and a skunk. Restaurants and grocery stores supplied leftovers or out-dated food supplies to feed the animals.

The children were delighted by the monkey Clarence who was trained to sit on Clarence's shoulder while he tended the grounds. Riley retired in 1972 after forty-seven years as caretaker of the park and zoo. Most of the animals were then sent to a zoo in Pueblo, Colorado.

At about the same time as Delta started its zoo with the peacock, Grand Junction was given a howling ape named JoJo from the Sels-Floto Circus, a *Denver Post* enterprise. That was the beginning of the Lincoln Park Zoo.

The zoo expanded through the years with animals being donated by citizens and state wildlife officials who supplied coyotes, bears, and other wild animals. These creatures had been illegally captured when they were infants and reared until they were considered unmanageable. Long-term caretaker Larry Murphy recalled an African lion that had a bad habit of urinating on the feet of viewers at its cage.

There were also bears that shared cages adjoining a pool of water. They received fish from a local fishing contest and while they ate their prizes, learned to splash water on the spectators. One bear thought it so much fun that he jumped in to the shrieks of the totally soaked onlookers.

Lincoln Park's coyotes were usually silent unless a fire truck or police car sped down Twelfth Street with sirens screaming. Then the coyotes would join the chorus with their famous howls. One African lion, raised from birth in captivity, would often roar into the late evening, much to the consternation of nearby residents.

A monkey named "Happy" escaped his cage one summer day and managed to get into the park's golf cart shed where he intimidated the golfers who entered. On another occasion, a skunk escaped and took refuge in the concession stand, which had to be flooded to drive him out.

Despite a favorable report in 1968 by the Colorado Board of Animal Protection, several citizens began to feel that the inhabitants of Lincoln Park Zoo should be given their freedom. The nationwide trend was for zoos to provide large ranging areas for the animals, but there was neither space nor money for such a zoo in Grand Junction. By 1970, most of the animals had been transferred to the Delta Zoo.

THE RISE AND FALL
OF A PHILANTHROPIST

*An Ironic Twist of Fate
for W.J. Moyer*

W.J. Moyer was born in Reading, Pennsylvania, in 1858. After working in the retail business in several states, he arrived in Grand Junction in 1890 and founded what was probably the largest mercantile store in Grand Junction, "The Fair." By 1910, it was located in his two-story building on the southeast corner of Fifth and Main Streets.

Moyer and his wife built a beautiful home at 620 North Seventh Street, now designated an historic preservation area. The Fair was very successful and led to other investments, such as Moyer's leadership in establishing the Grand Valley National Bank — then tallest structure in town — on the opposite corner from his store.

The Moyers were childless, but very generous to the youth of the city. They paid for college educations of at least eighteen young men. Moyer donated land on Colorado Avenue for the original Salvation Army store and later helped establish the Young Men's Christian Association. Their greatest philanthropy was the donation of a public swimming pool in Lincoln Park, since known as the Moyer Natatorium. It provided free swimming for children on Wednesdays and Saturdays.

During the peak years, The Fair had forty-four employees, but Moyer was said to be losing his grip on good management practices. He made an investment in a huge apple production business that never showed a profit. His most serious misfortune was in financing many large loans to area cattlemen who were hit hard by the plunge in beef prices following World War I. When Mrs. Moyer died in 1926, the aging merchant lost his desire to fight off competition, and, with the stock market crash of 1929, The Fair went bankrupt. In 1933, the Grand Valley Bank closed down. It was later re-established as the First National Bank. Moyer lost everything, including his home.

Moyer was given a free room at the St. Regis Hotel by owner Harry Burnett, and other old friends also helped the destitute former civic leader. Several friends convinced the city to make W.J. the "manager" of Moyer Natatorium at seventy-five dollars per month, indeed a bitter irony, but it was enough to pay his expenses. He later fell and broke his hip, causing him to lie helpless until his death in 1943.

TEACHER AND SCHOOL
BUS DRIVER WHO DAMMED
THE AMERICAN WEST

Aspinall's Legacy

Born near Palisade in 1896, Wayne Aspinall would eventually become one of the most influential U.S. Congressmen in western Colorado history. His life has been well documented as the promoter of dams built throughout the Upper Colorado River basin, including the huge Glen Canyon Dam in Utah, which created Lake Powell.

After marrying a local sweetheart, Julia Kuhns, in 1920, Aspinall was a teacher of history and other social studies at Palisade High School. He also drove a school bus, owned a farm and orchard, attained a law degree, and became a member of the Palisade town board. By 1933, he was also a state legislator.

In 1946 Wayne Aspinall was elected to the United States House of Representatives, and he was re-elected eleven times, serving until 1972. In that time he not only created dozens of water reclamation projects, but was influential in the development and control of uranium production as well as national forest management.

He was not without his detractors, including many environmentalists. He was proud of the fact that a billion dollars had been spent in his Fourth Congressional District in dam construction. On the other hand, this was regarded as pure "pork barrel spending" by his opponents.

In his early campaigning, Aspinall would leave a little sign with the design popular in World War II stating "Kilroy Was Here" at every town he visited. His sign stated "Aspinall Was Here."

Julia died in 1969, and Wayne married another high school sweetheart, Essie Jeffers, in 1970. After leaving congress in 1972, Aspinall continued to be influential in state and national affairs. In July of 1983, Essie died, and a few months later Wayne passed on, a victim of prostate cancer. His legacy is evident in the many dams and diversion projects he sponsored throughout western Colorado. Almost everywhere one travels, there is evidence that "Aspinall Was Here!" A detailed account of his career can be found in Steve C. Schulte's book, *Wayne Aspinall and the Shaping of the American West.*

THE GREAT RAINBOW INVASION

The Doubling of Delta County Population

The Rainbows, a group of "hangovers" and newly enchanted from the 1960s hippie era, find a place to gather in the National Forests every Fourth of July weekend. In 1992, more than 20,000 of the so-called "Rainbow Family" showed up for the twenty-first annual meeting at Overland Reservoir, about ten miles north of Paonia, which at that time had a population of about 1,400.

Since it was set up on Gunnison National Forest land, the camp was legal but required dozens of military trench latrines, water purification devices, and hundreds of tons of trucked-in food. The "Rainbow Family" began to arrive in late June, some by hitchhiking, others arriving in private airplanes. The group ranges from forty-year-olds with PhDs to teenagers born much too late to remember the Woodstock era.

The realization that Paonia and Delta Counties were the destination for the event rather shocked the local residents, even though reports from past Rainbow gatherings indicated that "peace, love, and healing" were usually the only activities. At the campsite, such places as the "Quit-Yer-Bitchin'-Love-Light-Kitchen" served oatmeal, as well as offering "free food, free love, free smoke."

Paonia and Delta Counties braced for the onslaught and established a central Incident Command post at the local high school. State highway patrolmen were told to ticket even the slightest traffic violations without "profiling" drivers. Thus a number of long-time Delta County residents were stopped for violations for which they had never previously been ticketed.

Health and sanitation inspections of the camp were routine and strict. There was a huge demand for federal food stamps from evidently impoverished visitors. Some panhandled on the streets of

Paonia and at least one stripped nude in the Laundromat while his clothes were being washed. Some, when realizing business restrooms were not for public use, resorted to alleys for their relief.

During the week at camp, one woman died in her tent from the fumes of a gasoline or kerosene lantern. Others came down with various ailments and were treated by a Rainbow medical team; and some were sent to the Delta hospital.

Some veteran Rainbows claimed Paonia was the least friendly town they had encountered. At the end of the celebration, some of the participants stayed on until the grounds were cleaned and restored as closely as possible to the original condition. A few stayed longer, taking up residence in Delta County, finding useful jobs, and even creating businesses of their own.

Getting
Educated

CHEWING GUM DAY
AT LINCOLN SCHOOL

Profile of a Principal

Lincoln School (now Lincoln Orchard Mesa) was a two-room structure at 2888 B½ Road near Grand Junction in the 1920s. Beginning in 1925, and for the next decade, Julius Gigax was the principal and taught grades five through eight. His wife, Lula, taught the first four grades.

Julius was considered a fair but strict disciplinarian, as he delivered punishments ranging from reprimands to the judicious use of the strap in more serious misdemeanors such as bullying. Strappings were the common practice in those days, but Julius was often sent to other schools to temper the severe corporal punishment and mayhem allowed by other teachers. Julius and Lula became highly respected and loved by students and parents alike.

Julius was also known for adding festivals to the traditional holiday observances. One day in October, he would bring a trailer-load of watermelons from his own farm and all the students would enjoy the bounty of "Watermelon Day." January was for the "Sledding Holiday," when there was an evening sledding party on a hill near the Gigax farm. Julius' birthday in April was designated as "Chewing Gum Day," and all the students would be given gum several times during the day, merrily chomping all day through their classes. Chewing gum was absolutely forbidden on any other day. Then there was the popular annual "May Day" breakfast on May 1st, which was cooked and prepared by the teachers on outdoor campfires.

According to Eleanor M. Sealey, who wrote a history of the school, the academic standards were as high as the discipline was strict. In the required eighth-grade standard examinations for all rural schools in the county, there were ten from the Lincoln School who took the tests in 1934. Of those, three placed in the top ten in the county, and two others placed in the top five! Whether circumstances permitted the students to go to high school or not, there seems to have been no doubt that all Lincoln School graduates qualified for higher education.

"MR. JUNIOR COLLEGE"

The Leadership of the Wubbens

Horace Wubben was a remarkable leader. During the twenty-six years he served as president of Mesa Junior College, he cultivated a reputation for excellence and he became known in national educators' meetings as "Mr. Junior College."

Mesa was one of the two original junior colleges established in Colorado, both in 1925. The other was at Trinidad. When Wubben became president in 1937, the college moved from a downtown location to its current site on North Avenue and 12th Street in Grand Junction.

During his tenure, Wubben had a gift of finding highly qualified and talented faculty members. He never offered written contracts because his handshake as a gentleman sufficed, and there were no complaints about this custom throughout his tenure. He retired in December of 1963.

Mesa was primarily designed as a transfer junior college where students would be admitted to four-year institutions as juniors. A study at the University of Colorado in the 1950s showed Mesa transfer students

Horace Wubben, President of Mesa State College. 1956 yearbook photo.

attained higher grades in the upper-division studies than students enrolled in the University as freshmen.

By then, Mesa Junior College had become the place where national junior college accreditation teams came to establish standards for other transfer-oriented colleges. Mesa also offered two-year terminal programs, including practical nursing and law enforcement. Grand Junction was chosen as host to the National Junior College baseball tournament (later named the JUCO World Series), and it continues there decades after Mesa became a four-year college.

Horace's wife, Irene Wubben, was also a significant contributor to the culture of the region as she developed the Mesa County Library System by gradually combining the services of various public libraries. She promoted early childhood reading, and the main county library's children's section was named in her honor.

JOB CORPS SUCCESS

Despite Some Homesickness

The Collbran Job Corps opened in 1965 and furnished a fresh start for many needy young men, and later, women. As the first recruits were mostly from urban areas, they were somewhat bewildered at the isolated location of the new camp. They had, for the most part, come from poverty-stricken backgrounds and had had little, if any, medical care before joining the Corps. Some even feared inoculation.

Modeled on the 1930s' Civilian Conservation Corps, the program teaches useful skills and also has high school equivalency courses. Several recruits were sent home because they could not cope with homesickness, but the dropout rate at Collbran has been about average for the National Job Corps — twenty percent. The Collbran Center has received numerous citations for its effective operation.

QUILTS FOR GRADUATES

A Gateway Tradition

Since 1979, it has been the charming custom for each graduate at Gateway High School to be given a quilt. Members of the Wayside Chapel, as well as friends and family, prepare each quilt, using the graduate's favorite colors. An appropriate Bible verse is embroidered on each quilt, based on the individual graduate's interest. It is hoped this unusual custom continues on for all the future graduates of Gateway.

WHERE TALENT IS ENHANCED

The Western Colorado Math and Science Center

A unique supplement to public school education in this region is the Western Colorado Math and Science Center on Unaweep Avenue in Grand Junction. There, students ranging from elementary school on up can have hands-on experiences and learn from volunteer instructors in many aspects of the physical, natural, and even theoretical sciences.

It was founded by John McConnell, a retired scientist who felt there was much to offer in supplementing regular public school  education. His efforts attracted other retirees and volunteers. Space was provided by the school district in the New Emerson Elementary School and funding for supplies and equipment was furnished by donations from individuals and organizations. Thousands of youths visit the center every year to have their imagination stimulated by this program.

John McConnell was a mentor to a gifted senior at Central High School, Ryan Patterson. Ryan designed and built a glove that translates the American Sign Language alphabet into characters on a small computer screen, lessening the need for translators for the deaf. Ryan had won many first places in various science competitions, but in 2002 this invention earned the coveted first place in both the National Siemens Westinghouse Science and Technology Competition and the Young Scientist Award from Intel, considered the equivalent of a "Junior Nobel Prize." He was ranked first in *Forbes* magazine's ASAP's High Tech All-American Team. He was greeted and welcomed by the President of the United States and continued on a scholarship at the University of Colorado. His accomplishment brought national recognition to this successful achievement and McConnell's inspired vision.

Medical
Matters

SECOND INCOMES FOR DOCTORS

Farming, Bootlegging, and Counterfeiting

A century ago, most rural medical doctors were highly respected, but also poorly compensated for the services they provided. Mesa and Delta Counties' doctors usually received fifty cents for an office call, and some services might be paid for with a chicken, some eggs, or other produce. Patients were rarely billed; it was understood they would pay when and if they could. Late one night, a Paonia doctor rode ten miles to an outlying ranch where he performed an emergency appendectomy, using the kitchen table as an operating table. He received five dollars for his services.

Several doctors went into farming to supplement their meager incomes. A group of doctors diverted irrigation water to what is still known as Doctors' Mesa, west of Eckert. At least one doctor ran a still out in the adobe lands and then prescribed and sold strong medicine to knowing "patients" who were not necessarily ill.

Another physician, Dr. Eggleton of Eckert, owned engraving and printing equipment and was successful for a few years in counterfeiting money. He spent so much of his phony money that he was finally arrested. President Theodore Roosevelt was petitioned for a pardon, but none was forthcoming. Finally, federal agents declared Eggleston insane, and he was sent to an asylum for the rest of his life.

THE DIPHTHERIA DANCE

Anatomy of an Epidemic

One of the most dreaded diseases in the early half of the Twentieth Century was diphtheria. Highly contagious, it often resulted in death within twenty-four hours.

In Escalante Canyon west of Delta, the ranchers often held dances in the schoolhouse. It was usual for the adults to bring small children who, as they grew tired, would be bedded down to sleep in the corner, where desks and benches had been pushed to clear the floor for dancing.

On a Saturday night in March of 1923, at one such dance, there were several people in attendance who had sore throats. One was the schoolteacher, Miss Millie Simineo, who didn't dance much as she wasn't feeling well. Two little boys got sleepy very early and were tucked away. The dance went on until almost sun-up the next morning.

On Monday morning, Miss Simineo wasn't able to open school. The people, with whom she boarded, Bert and Emma Shreeves, sent for Delta's noted doctor, Winfield Scott Cleland (Cleland Park was later named for him). By the time he reached the house, Sonny, the five year-old son of the Shreeves, was also ill, the membranes in his throat beginning to choke him.

Dr. Cleland stayed on overnight, and, by morning, Miss Simineo was dead. The doctor knew the cause to be diphtheria. Sonny died, and three other children later succumbed, despite the fact that Dr. Cleland had a rider gallop to Delta for vaccine with which he injected all of the partygoers.

The Shreeves house was fumigated with formaldehyde, but the vapor failed to penetrate some bedding stored in trunks. The school was deliberately burned to the ground with all its contents. Some adults who contracted the disease went to Delta and were quarantined.

The following August, the Shreeves moved up to their cow camp on the Uncompahgre Plateau, taking the blankets from the trunk with them. Their six-year-old daughter, Wilma, slept in the blankets, and soon thereafter died from the disease. Rumors abounded throughout Delta, and terror took over when anyone was late in returning from a trip. In all, at least a dozen people died out of forty or more who contracted the disease. Two people died not of the disease, but of an allergic reaction to the horse serum used in preparing the antitoxin. The best-detailed account of this tragedy may be found in the late Muriel Marshall's book, *Red Hole in Time.*

PHYSICIAN, ROCKHOUND, RUG COLLECTOR

The Remarkable Career of Dr. Gould in Paonia and Grand Junction

A.H. "Arch" Gould was born in 1903 in Arkansas, the oldest of eight children of a cotton farmer. When he was eight years old, Arch decided he wanted to become a missionary doctor when he grew up.

After many sacrifices, he was able to graduate from high school and the College of the Ozarks, where he received honors. Before long, he fell in love and married Alice Lee, and the two moved to Cleveland, Ohio, where Arch started medical studies at Case Western Reserve University. He worked as an elevator operator at a hotel and at various other jobs in order to pay his expenses. Alice joined him in selling blood, and even pawned her wedding ring. It was finally decided that Alice should go to Paonia to live with relatives in order to save living costs, while, as an advanced student, Arch was able to deliver babies for a fee.

Arch finally got his M.D. degree in 1934 and drove a battered Model T Ford west. He had a job interview in South Dakota, but took a detour to pick up Alice in Paonia. The long-time and only doctor in Paonia, Dr. Hazlett, was ready to retire and wanted to sell his practice. It was agreed it would be a great opportunity for Arch, so Alice's uncle co-signed a note for $5,000 to pay for the office and home located on the northeast corner of Second and Onarga Streets.

On the first day that Arch opened his doors, a seven-year-old swallowed a cherry pit, which lodged in his esophagus. There were none of the sophisticated devices for extraction such as had existed in Cleveland, so Arch called Dr. Hazlett, who advised him to inject apomorphine to induce vomiting. Arch gave the injection, and then realized he had given an adult dose rather than one for children. The child screamed and threw up violently, but survived and the pit was extracted. This was Arch Gould's introduction to small town medical practice.

Archibald Gould.   Courtesy of Anne Gould

The following Sunday, he received a message that a boy was very ill at the small community of Pilot's Knob, which could only be reached by horseback up Hubbard Creek. The lad was suffering from calcium deficiency, having had no milk all winter. Gould noticed the cabin had been caulked with lime, and he scratched out some powder, mixed it with water, and, after drinking the brew, the boy felt well within hours. On another occasion, he noted that a child was doing fine on peanut butter mixed with water at another isolated home where they had run out of canned milk.

A dentist, Dr. Louis Bradshaw, joined the practice and brought along an X-ray machine for both of the men to use. Soon Arch was delivering babies at isolated ranches and performing operations on kitchen tables. It was reported that he placed "blue babies" in ovens to help them survive.

Mine accidents killed an average of three men a year in Dr. Gould's area and many times he was able to give the on-the-spot treatment essential for recovery. On one occasion he spent three days at the Juanita Mine in Bowie, which had caught fire, causing many burn injuries.

When a small hospital was opened in Hotchkiss, Arch became a staff member. On one occasion, a young boy in Paonia had a very serious appendicitis attack, but the family refused to let Arch take him to the hospital where they said, "people go to die." With the help of Dr. Hazlett in administering ether, Gould operated. The patient recovered, but Arch said, "My own recovery was rough."

A miner contracted meningitis, and sulpha drugs provided no relief. Arch made national headlines when he telephoned to Boston for a vial of the still-experimental penicillin. It was flown to Denver, and the Colorado Highway Patrol rushed it to Paonia. That was the first use of penicillin in Colorado, and it saved the patient's life.

During the Depression years, Dr. Gould was often paid with such items as fruit, potatoes, chickens, or venison. Until World War II ended, he never charged more than two dollars for an office visit.

In 1947, the family moved to Grand Junction, where he continued to expand on his notable reputation. Arch and Alice divorced in 1964 and the next year he married Anne Holden. In 1968, at the age of sixty-five, he "retired," and was able to realize his childhood dream by donating his services in caring for Navajo Indians in Utah and Arizona. He also began collecting rocks and Indian rugs.

Taking part in the CARE program, he was sent to Alaska, the Aleutian Islands, Kenya, and Honduras. In all of these places he was able to rely on the skills he learned in Paonia, as almost all of his assignments were in isolated regions with little modern equipment.

Picking up rocks all over the world, Arch had a very special collection, which he later gave to Mesa College. His rug collection was representative of natives from all over the world. The collection included over 250 rugs and many were eventually donated to various museums throughout the country, including the Western Colorado Center for the Arts in Grand Junction.

A.H. "Arch" Gold died in 1990, leaving thousands of grateful families, and the world a better place.

DR. GENO: TRACER OF
CANCER CELLS

Exploding the Myth that Grand Junction was "A Doomed City"

It is impossible to estimate how many lives have been saved by the early detection method of lung cancer created by the late Dr. Geno Saccomanno of Grand Junction.

He established a pathology laboratory at St. Mary's Hospital in 1947 and served the needs of the local Veterans Administration Hospital. A native of Spring Glen, near Price, Utah, he had served as an instructor in pathology at St. Louis University.

During his career, he studied sputum samples of 17,500 miners and also cadavers of lung cancer victims. As a result, he found that the samples showed cancer long before any tumors showed up in x-rays. After a long struggle with the nationwide medical establishment, his findings revolutionized cancer diagnosis.

As a center of uranium mining and processing during the post World War II boom, Grand Junction was the ideal place to study the relationship between underground mining radiation, cigarette smoking, and cancer. Because low-level radiation in 300,000 tons of tailings from the Climax uranium mill had been used widely over the region for everything from landscaping to construction, the issue had become a center of controversy.

The Atomic Energy Commission was accused of underestimating the radiation's effects. At a public meeting on the question, one official pointed out that there was "no more danger than from the luminous hands and numbers on your wristwatch."

In 1970, *McCall's* magazine published an article, "America's Most Radioactive City," which implied that many people would, over the next twenty years, either leave the Grand Valley or suffer cancer as a result of radon gas from the tailings. Other shocking

Geno Saccomanno, Ph.D., M.D., 1915-1999.
Photograph courtesy of the *Daily Sentinel.*

stories were carried in major newspapers across the nation. Locally, very few people seemed to be seriously worried.

Enter the Environmental Protection Agency with a vast program to remove the tailings. As this effort would employ many people, involve railroad and truck transportation, and require a special paved highway with an overpass crossing Highway 50 between Delta and Grand Junction, it was a welcome relief. The "oil shale boom" of the 1970s had become a bust in 1982, and the economy was devastated.

In the meantime Dr. Saccomanno continued his research and found that non-smokers who lived in homes where radon gas was evident were not contracting cancer as predicted. The EPA was promoting a nationwide alert on radon dangers, but, in 1994, Dr.

GRAND MESA COUNTRY

Saccomanno could point out that the radiation level was very low and that "the biggest crime of it all is [the EPA] trying to foist this $40 billion cost on the public…. They have no evidence to justify this."

Dr. Saccomanno had also invented a brush wash plastic tube to secure sputum samples. This invention was well received by the medical world. He donated all its proceeds to St. Mary's Hospital. With two authoritative books and more than ninety-five scholarly papers to his credit, Saccomanno became world-famous, and doctors as far away as Japan came to consult with him.

He and his wife, Virginia, raised three children in Grand Junction. Among Geno's hobbies was playing the stock market. He founded the Saccomanno Education Center and donated $2.5 million to a scholarship foundation for students from Mesa County and his original home, Carbon County, Utah. The Saccomanno Research Institute was also created for continuing research on lung cancer. His contribution to many public projects and organizations are still remembered. He passed away in 1999 at the age of eighty-two.

Sporting
and Other
Challenges

TWO BULLDOG TALES

Palisade's Jack and Trolley Car Boots

Early in the 1920s, a great fan of the Palisade baseball team, Mr. Marion Brown, brought his bulldog, Jack, to the local games. The team seemed to win whenever Jack was there to bark for them. As he was considered a lucky charm, Jack became the mascot for all sports at the high school. In 1992, Scott Shaffer created a statue of the dog, and it became a fixture in the entryway at Palisade High School. Students seemed to feel the name "Jack" wasn't ferocious enough and began calling the bulldog "Spike," probably inspired by the collar design on the statue.

Also in the early 1920s, a white bulldog named Boots learned to wait at the corner of Seventh Street and Gunnison Avenue in Grand

Jack — Palisade Bulldog

Junction. This was a regular stop on the electric trolley service at the time. Often when the trolley car stopped, Boots would board it and ride down to the main street near the jewelry store of his master, Frank Blackstone, where he got off the car. Usually after his visit Boots would make it home by paw power, although some say he also learned to freeload on the trolley for the return trip home.

GRAND JUNCTION THRILLED
BY BARNSTORMERS

Barney Oldfield vs. Barnstormer Beachy in a Race

In 1912, Grand Junction witnessed its first airplane demonstration. It was reported that a crowd of 5,000 showed up at the fairgrounds (now Lincoln Park) to watch barnstormer Charles Walsh fly his Curtis biplane — dipping, turning, and suddenly rising in the air.

The event was promoted by Walter Walker, publisher of the *Daily Sentinel*, and residents were warned to keep horses away from Twelfth Street and North Avenue to prevent stampeding. Excursion trains brought enthusiasts from Montrose and Fruita.

While advances were being made in "aeroplanes," remarkable improvements took place in automobile engineering. Bernard Oldfield, more popularly known as "Barney Oldfield," was America's most famous racing car driver and the first man to reach the speed of a mile a minute at the Indianapolis Speedway.

Barney was thirty-six years old on October 10, 1914, when he made a visit to Grand Junction and met noted flier Lincoln Beachy. They challenged each other to a contest, plane vs. auto, and the race was staged at the fairgrounds. Barney won the race by thirty feet, but Beachy compensated by looping his plane five times, and flying low and upside down over the heads of the spectators.

TENNIS AND CROQUET UNDER THE RIM OF GRAND MESA

Opening of the Mesa Lakes Resort

In June of 1891, W.J. Moore opened the Mesa Lakes Resort, on the shoulder of Grand Mesa. It was considered by a Grand Junction newspaper as "without any doubt the finest natural resort in the state." The resort had a hotel, several cabins, and tents available, and also boasted of having "frequent catches" of trout weighing two pounds or more.

The resort could be reached from the town of DeBeque, where trains were scheduled from both east and west during the noon hour every day. Bert Strout's "finest tourist wagon west of the range" would meet the trains and take tourists to Mesa Lakes, seventeen miles away. Using relays of horses, the trip could be made in four hours.

Among the attractions in the "primitive forest" were a tennis court and croquet grounds.

KING TUT AND
THE FIRST BANK NIGHT

Delta's Egyptian Theatre

It was in 1922 that two British archaeologists discovered the first intact tomb of an Egyptian pharaoh, Tutankhamen, who has since come to be called "King Tut." The splendors of the artifacts found there were instrumental in creating a new rage of imitating the ancient culture, including a taste for such architectural style in numerous movie theaters in America.

When Consolidated Theaters in Denver decided to build a new movie palace in Delta, they opted for the Egyptian style and they named the theater "Egyptian," a moniker it still holds today.

With seating for 750 people, it was Colorado's most up-to-date theater when it opened. Stucco details of Egyptian busts, hieroglyphs, and other symbols graced the walls. It had a glassed-in "cry room" where noisy babies could be taken while allowing mothers to watch the movie. First-run movies were shown there for thirty-five cents. Some movie stars showed up in person on stage, including Mae West, Tom Mix, and Greta Garbo.

What made the Egyptian most famous, however, was the brainchild of either district manager Charles Yeager or Delta manager Frank Ricketson. During the Great Depression years of the 1930s, twenty local merchants were asked to donate five dollars each for a grand sum of a hundred dollars, which was then to be given to one movie patron in a lottery drawing. One hundred dollars was a significant prize and people from out of town would flock to Delta, patronizing other stores in town on the day of the drawings.

This promotion became known as "Bank Night," and was usually held on Wednesday of each week. Soon the Egyptian was drawing the highest box office receipts of any of the company's twenty-eight theaters. Prizes grew, including free dinnerware, groceries, a

Egyptian Theatre Delta.

radio, and even a Ford car. There was additional entertainment on Bank Night, with sing-alongs, local dancers, or amateur performers.

The idea swept the nation, and soon thousands of theaters were featuring Bank Nights. All good things have to come to an end, though, and by 1938, the federal government put a stop to these illegal lotteries.

As the years went on, some of the Egyptian decorations fell into disrepair; then the façade of the building was modernized. In 1995, state historical association preservation experts, at the invitation of the local historical society, found that beneath the walls that had been covered with thin concrete, the original decorations could be found. With careful work, the Egyptian was restored to its former glory, partly financed by a Colorado Historical Society grant.

"THE LONGEST DISTANCE
BETWEEN TWO POINTS"

*Building and Racing on the
Lands End Road*

It has been recorded that the Land's End Road on the steep western drop-off of Grand Mesa was originally an Indian trail. John Otto, founder of the Colorado National Monument, improved it in the 1920s. In 1933, the federal government decided to make it into an automobile road. Assigned to the job was a company of World War I veterans, a special adjunct to the Civilian Conservation Corps. The route was originally called the "Veterans' Road."

Work was done mostly by hand labor and was completed within one year. It had so many "zigzags" that a race driver once called it "the longest distance between two points."

In 1940, Louis Unser, who had been a winner of the famous Pike's Peak Hill Climb many times, brought his racing car to Land's End for a trial. He declared it the most challenging such racecourse in the nation. Salt Lake City Mayor Ab Jenkins, who held more auto racing medals than anyone else, secured an American Automobile Association endorsement for a race and came to conduct the contest.

Among the entrants were two French "wheel-benders" who brought their six-cylinder 259 horsepower cars across the Atlantic to compete. The finish line was 5,000 feet above the starting line point, traveling fourteen and a half miles to go seven miles as a crow flies. Unser's car smashed up in the second mile; his Colorado Springs friend Al Rodgers won the contest.

In the second race held July 4, 1941, Unser won the contest in seventeen minutes, eleven and a half seconds. Hundreds of spectators watched almost the entire race from the rim above the course. World War II brought an end to what was to have been annual, AAA-sanctioned contests, but since that time there have been annual races conducted by local enthusiasts.

Ad in the Grand Junction's Daily Sentinel, *June 20, 1982.*

A WORLD CHAMPION
WEIGHTLIFTER

Grand Junction's Juanita Trujillo

When Juanita Trujillo was a student at Grand Junction High School, she became outstanding in the field events of shot put and discus. After graduating in 1983, she trained in power lifting, and, by 1986, Juanita won the world championship in the women's 90-Kilo division of that sport. The world finals were held in Jonkopina, Sweden.

Juanita went to Mesa State College, getting a B.S. degree in Biology in 1990. In 1992, she returned to the weightlifting finals, this time in the 90-Kilo Plus division, and gained her second world championship at the age of twenty-two.

BRIDGE CHAMPIONS

Twenty-Fifth Place in World Competition

Partners in a duplicate bridge club in Grand Junction were surprised to find out that they ranked twenty-fifth out of 100,000 teams worldwide. The World Bridge Federation, with headquarters in Memphis, Tennessee, conducted the contest in July of 2003.

Fran Paiva and Marilyn McLaughlin, long-time players in the Bridge 'n More Club, scored a sixty-six percent win, just under the "perfect score" of seventy percent. Local directors deal contestants worldwide the same hands. Afterwards the game scores were verified and reported.

Mrs. Paiva is a former teacher of algebra and later founded Driver Education Schools in four different cities. She has been playing bridge for half a century. Mrs. McLaughlin worked in the medical field and the real estate business at Vail until she and her husband bought Grand Junction's A-1 Driver School from Fran Paiva.

One wonders if they can read each other's mind while bidding.

They Took Pen in Hand

AGRICULTURAL WRITER
WHO FOUNDED FRUITA

Pabor Was Also a Poet Laureate

Born in New York City in 1834, William E. Pabor was a writer for Horace Greeley's *New York Tribune* following the Civil War. He was a friend of the agricultural editor of that newspaper, Nathan C. Meeker. Meeker, dismayed by the corrupt postwar culture, persuaded Christian farmers to form a socialist colony on the South Platte River in Colorado. That colony was known as the Union Colony, which later became the town of Greeley. It was a dream that evaporated within three years, and Meeker later tried his hand as a Ute Indian Agent, working with the "noble savages." He failed miserably at this occupation and was killed by the Utes in the 1879 "Meeker Massacre."

William Pabor, founder of Fruita, Colorado.
Carol Knapp drawing courtesy Loyd Files Research Library, Museum of Western Colorado, 1992.25.

Pabor served as secretary of Meeker's Union Colony. When that venture failed, he helped General Palmer establish Colorado Springs, and may have been involved in the founding of Fort

Collins. In 1883, Pabor wrote the first book on farming in Colorado: *Colorado as an Agricultural State.* He was also associate editor of the *Colorado Farmer* publication and Secretary of the Colorado State Press Association.

That same year, he arrived in the Grand Valley and saw the potential for fruit and other agriculture. He founded the town of Fruita, built its first house, and lived there with his wife and five children. William was by that time nearly fifty years old but was still a vigorous farmer, planting vegetables, flowers, and apple trees. His health declined, and he was forced to leave Fruita and move to a lower altitude. The family settled in Florida, where William founded another town, Pabor Lake, and a newspaper named *The Pineapple.*

During the later part of his life, he wrote and published books of poetry and was designated the Poet Laureate of the National Editorial Association. On a visit to Fruita in 1911, he died from a fit of apoplexy. His funeral at the local Methodist Church was one of the largest in the history of western Colorado, with 600 school children marching alongside the cortege to Elmwood Cemetery.

ONE OF THE FIRST BOOKS
PUBLISHED IN DELTA COUNTY

A Defense of the Sand Creek Massacre

Most historians regard the early dawn massacre of at least 150 Indians at Sand Creek in November 1864 as one of the worst blots on the history of Colorado. The Cheyenne tribe had been promised safe haven by Governor John Evans. A majority of the men in the tribe were away hunting at the time, so the victims were mostly women, children, and old men who had already hoisted a white flag. Colonel John M. Chivington, who led the attack by the Third Colorado Volunteer Regiment, was court-martialed as a result of the atrocious actions. President Lincoln fired Governor Evans, who was believed to have been involved in planning the deliberate deception of the Indians, and the ensuing encounter at Sand Creek helped touch off a series of Plains Indian wars which continued for years following the Civil War.

Luella Shaw wrote a defense of the massacre in her book *True History of Some of the Pioneers of Colorado.* It was published in Hotchkiss in 1909 by three veterans of the Colorado Third. In it, atrocities performed by several tribes of Indians themselves are given in detail, and there is actually a defense for the killing of children. The trial of Chivington is described as a sham — the manipulation of junior officers who coveted his office. The book contains other accounts that included buffalo hunts, early gold mining, outlaw activities, and other encounters with "the savage tribes." It is a rare collector's item today.

OUR EARLIEST COWBOY POET

Austin Corcoran's Adventurous and Literary Life

When Grand Junction was founded officially in 1882, Austin Corcoran's family moved there from Pennsylvania. Austin was only two-years-old, one of ten children. As he later remembered, "I lived most of my life on the edge of civilization."

Whenever it was convenient, Austin was sent to the local school, and he was quick to learn the power of words. As a teenager he served as a guide for the survey party that claimed to have given the name "Bookcliffs" to that range. Up river, the expedition found a Henry rifle by a stream and named the stream Rifle Creek. The subsequent settlement became the town of Rifle.

At the age of nineteen, Austin went off to seek his fortune in the Alaskan Gold Rush. That did not fulfill his hopes, so he boarded a ship bound for Hawaii where he got a job herding cattle. Then he went to Mexico and continued his cowboy career. After a year, he returned to the Grand Valley and established a homestead, got married, and began a family.

Austin Corcoran became one of the first, if not the first, cowboy poets with the publication of his "Chuck Time on the Roundup" in a popular magazine in 1915. This led to other poems and short stories in magazines that were included in anthologies. In 1928, Austin sold his land and cattle and devoted his whole time to writing. Such magazines as *Collier's* and *The Saturday Evening Post* were fascinated with this writer who was a real western cowboy. His most popular poems included "Silver Saddles," "Medicine Ranch," and "Walls of Thunder Creek." Austin later moved to Cañon City, where he wrote a full volume of poetry entitled *Hidden Trails*. It was published in 1962, a short time before his death at the age of eighty-seven.

CATTLE, SHEEP, AND
KANNAH CREEK

The Adventures of Louis Farmer

Louis Farmer was born in 1901 on a cattle ranch on Kannah Creek near the town of Whitewater. He spent most of his life either there, or on Grand Mesa, or in the summer alpine grazing areas around Aspen and Crested Butte. When he was over eighty years old, Louis wrote down his many adventures as a cattleman and sheepman. He also included a number of original poems.

The resulting book was *Snowbound in the High Rockies and Other True Short Stories,* 200 pages of tales about people, animals, and places worth sharing. His memory stretched back to early child-hood and his education at the one-room Pride School.

Leading the series is a bone-chilling story of a crisis on a mountain pass, "Two Men, Five Dogs, One Horse, Four Mules, and Three-Thousand Sheep." Other adventures involve loyal dogs, terror on a dark night on Grand Mesa when a bear or mountain lion stalked him, dynamiting prairie dog towns, and racing in a wagon carrying a corpse to meet a train at Whitewater. Published in 1985, the book is available at several area libraries. Louis died in 1990.

SHEPHERD, PHOTOGRAPHER, NATURALIST, PHILOSOPHER

This Man Knew His Coyotes!

Will C. Minor herded sheep for thirty-five years on Pinion Mesa, Glade Park, and as high up as the towering Mosquito Range near Leadville. He also wrote two volumes of some of the best stories about animals, birds, insects, trees, and other aspects of nature that he had the time to observe in his career.

Born in Missouri, his family moved to Colorado in 1904 when he was a toddler. Will arrived in Fruita as a young man already established as a published writer, having sold his first story to *Boys Life* when he was sixteen years old. Through the years, he wrote for many other publications, mainly outdoor magazines.

Will Minor.
Courtesy of the *Daily Sentinel,* 1972.

He was also a photographer, using a simple box camera to capture pictures of wild animals. He sold many of these by mail and others were used to illustrate his articles. Will was also a collector of butterflies. He discovered a new species, which was then named for him: papilio indra minori.

His greatest fascination was with coyotes. He was probably one of the most knowledgeable experts on coyotes to be found anywhere. He did not believe any coyote trap worked — the creatures were too clever. He had set many traps over the years, but the coyotes never were caught. The coyotes killed many sheep, so Will resorted to shooting many of them. Nevertheless, he believed that coyotes were smart enough to know about rifles, and whenever they spotted a rifle they would stay hidden but would cavort openly in front of an unarmed man. Thus he came to respect the wily predator. In *Footprints in the Trail,* Will wrote:

> *Coyotes are cowards. That is what most men who should be in a position to know will tell you. They may be right. But who among us is qualified, when speaking of wild animals, to say just where cowardice stops and wisdom begins? The dividing line between the two is sometimes very thin indeed. It is all very well for men who have guns and other deadly weapons at their command to call an animal that keeps out of sight a coward. But perhaps it is wisdom rather than cowardice. If the odds were even, it might be a different matter.*

Will's writings were laced with many other examples of a philosophic approach to the natural world he so loved. His original book was so popular that another followed it: *More Footprints in the Trail.*

The good shepherd died in Grand Junction in 1981 at the age of seventy-eight but his unique insights and observations live on.

A COMEDY SET IN "SHALE CITY" COLORADO

It was Performed Worldwide

An undertaker and a newspaper publisher are awaiting the death of a very wealthy man. The undertaker has an option on the most expensive coffin in the state and wants to get it before Olinger's Mortuary in Denver grabs it. The newspaper will have a "scoop" on news so important that it will affect the stock markets. They rush up and get the body, only to realize the man is not quite dead after all. The rest of the play is hilarious enough to keep audiences laughing throughout.

The play is named "The Biggest Thief in Town" and is set in Shale City, playwright Dalton Trumbo's name for Grand Junction, the city in which he grew up. Opening in 1949, it played in several U.S. cities, had a long run in London, Canada, Netherlands, Rome, South Africa, and Australia. It is still being staged by amateur groups and has been performed in Colorado, including Gunnison and Montrose, but not in Grand Junction (as of this writing).

The play opened on Broadway the same season as Arthur Miller's powerful tragedy "Death of a Salesman." The *New Yorker* magazine reviewer was shocked that a comedy about death was being staged nearby, and other reviewers agreed, closing Trumbo's show after only two weeks. However, in London, it ran for two years until one of the main actors died. Renewed off-Broadway in New York, it was once again a success with Zero Mostel (later famed for the lead role in "Fiddler on the Roof") playing the part of the undertaker.

A graduate of Grand Junction High School, Trumbo had been a cub reporter for the *Daily Sentinel* and covered death notices, spending much time at local mortuaries. He later wrote a novel published in London, *Eclipse*, which was a scathing indictment of Grand Junction as "Shale City." Trumbo went on to become perhaps the most famous Hollywood screenwriter of his time. Sentenced to ten months in jail because he refused to testify to the House Committee on Un-American Activities, he was banned from his career until actor Kirk Douglas revealed that Trumbo was the screenplay author of the movie *Spartacus*. Trumbo had been writing outstanding scripts under assumed names, one of which won an academy award for the unidentified author.

Trumbo may have had leftist leanings, but he was definitely a pacifist. His famous novel *Johnny Got His Gun* (later a movie) was a tragic account of a World War I soldier from Shale City, Colorado. Shale City was also the setting for another Trumbo novel and movie, *The Remarkable Andrew*. When he died in 1976, Trumbo had written the screenplays for fifty-eight films, eight novels and plays, and three works of non-fiction.

HOW TO HAVE A GOOD FUNERAL

Ed Martin's Successful Guide Book

Psychology of Funeral Service, first published in 1950, was a guide for morticians nationwide. By its sixth edition in 1977, 23,000 copies had been sold, perhaps a record for any book published in Grand Junction.

Author Edward A. Martin, born in 1902, had become heir to Martin's Mortuary, founded by his father, Fred C. Martin. Ed was an avid scholar, creative thinker, and a popular citizen of Grand Junction. His work is an outstanding, concise study of world religions, primitive rituals, symbolism, and modern attitudes toward death.

His guide to public relations in all aspects of the mortuary business is very detailed and includes insights into the wishes of survivors. He included now-common euphemisms, such as casket, not coffin; selection room, not showroom; service, not funeral; deceased, not dead; and other terms.

When author Jessica Mitford first published her best-selling book *The American Way of Death* in 1963, she attacked the role of morticians for promoting exorbitant funeral and burial costs,

Ed Martin's Mortuary

suggesting that the industry had gone far beyond what was proper and tasteful. Among her derogatory references was Ed Martin's book.

On the other hand, Ed's book has much to say about ethics and professional standards. Whether Ed created it himself or adapted it, he included a solemn "Funeral Service Oath" to which he felt all morticians should adhere. Ed retired, and his son, Paul, took over the mortuary. It has long since been sold to outside interests. Ed died in 1987.

A MAN OF MANY TALENTS

The Prolific Output of Al Look

Alfred Alvin Look lived ninety-six years and he managed to cram at least eleven careers into that time! Born in 1896, Al joined the U.S. Navy after graduating from the University of Nebraska, his home state, during World War I. Having majored in journalism, he was employed by a Durango, Colorado, newspaper in 1920. During that time he took a leave of absence to become a leading man in a silent movie filmed at Farmington, New Mexico. He homesteaded near Dove Creek, Colorado, while writing features for the Durango newspaper.

In 1923, Al came to Grand Junction to take the position of advertising manager for the *Daily Sentinel*. He married Margaret Langen, a schoolteacher from Ohio who would provide him with incentive and inspiration for well over half a century. His success in advertising led to national recognition and the publication of two books, *Advertising at Retail* and *No Advertising: 57 Ways Not to Advertise.* He also taught the subject at Grand Junction's Ross Business College.

Al Look

Al's interest in paleontology led to the discovery of a new species of dinosaur, named for him, Spractolamda Look. His explorations in archaeology resulted in two sites being named after him in Utah and Unaweep Canyon. His popular book on these subjects was first titled *In my Back Yard*, but a later edition bore the title *A Hundred Million Years on the Colorado Plateau.*

He was fascinated with Native American cultures and came to know many Indians as friends. Al wrote three books on the Ute Indians. One book, *Hopi Indian Snake Dance*, was based on a rare privilege granted to him and described a ceremony, which very few outsiders were allowed to witness.

Al was interested in all of Colorado and published two anecdotal books, *S'Fact and Sidelights on Colorado*, with his own illustrations. He wrote biographies of John Otto, founder of Colorado National Monument, and Harold Bryant, a prominent western artist. His book, *U-Boom*, was one of the first accounts of Colorado and Utah uranium prospecting and production.

He became a character in a nationally syndicated cartoon strip named *Don Winslow of the Navy*, which delved into stories of artifacts from the region. Al's own paintings of eight Indian chiefs were commissioned by a Pueblo, Colorado, movie theater. During much of his career, he wrote a humor column for the *Daily Sentinel.*

Before the days of radio, Al would broadcast, to the people gathered on the street, the incoming news of boxing matches, the World Series games, and other sporting events of national interest, reading the news fresh off the *Daily Sentinel's* teletype. He also wrote a section for the *Look Magazine* book publication titled "The Santa Fe Trail."

The Looks had a tradition that the day before Christmas, they bought all unsold toys from merchants at half price and then hosted a party at the Avalon Theater complete with candy and free toys for all who showed up. One year, 1,900 children went home with Christmas toys.

Though Al Look died in 1992, his works continue to be a source of enrichment for many people who never had a chance to know this exceptional man personally.

NORTH FORK'S FAMED HISTORIAN

The Prolific Wilson Rockwell

Wilson Rockwell owned a ranch near the town of Crawford, and was the son of the prominent former Lieutenant Governor and U.S. Congressman, Robert F. Rockwell. In addition to that, Wilson Rockwell was one of the most prolific historians of western Colorado. His book about the settlement and development of the North Fork of the Gunnison was titled *New Frontier*. He also wrote an exemplary work, *Uncompahgre Country*. Broadening his scope, his *Sunset Slope* told of exciting incidents throughout western Colorado. Interviewing the famous Gunnison County sheriff, Doc Shores, Wilson turned the adventurous life of that shrewd officer into an autobiographical style work, *Memoirs of a Lawman*. Wilson also turned his talents to creative writing, and his *No Way Back* was a successful novel. In addition to his books, he had a number of articles published in the *Colorado Magazine*, authoritative periodical of the Colorado Historical Society. Wilson also undertook painstaking research and much interviewing to write the definitive first treatment of the Indians of the region named *The Utes: A Forgotten People*. Today, it is still regarded as one of the best works on the subject and is in great demand in the out-of-print book market. Reprints of *The Utes, Sunset Slope*, and *Uncompahgre Country* are also selling well.

In 1969, when his son, Dan, was slated for draft into the military during the Vietnam War, Wilson Rockwell decided that actions speak louder than words. He relinquished his Colorado State Senate seat and moved to Creston, British Columbia, where he purchased a 240-acre ranch. Although he was a strong Republican, former Colorado State Senator, and former college classmate of President Nixon, he wrote Nixon: "I believe that this nation's Vietnam adventure will be recorded in history as the greatest and most costly mistake this country ever made."

While in Canada, Wilson wrote columns on the pioneers of his Creston Valley area and described the lifestyles of the Kootenai Indians who once lived there. In 1976, his book, *We Hold These Truths,* was published. It was an account of his decision to leave the United States and his new life in Canada. In 1994, he published *Creston Valley Profiles,* a history of that region.

Some of his manuscripts were given to the Paonia Library, and the Crawford Library has a room dedicated to the memory of his wife, Enid, who was instrumental in establishing the original collection there.

A PREMIER WRITER OF
WESTERN HISTORY

Delta's Agnes Wright Spring

Agnes Wright is in both the National Cowboy Hall of Fame and the National Cowgirl Hall of Fame. She has been the State Historian for both Colorado and Wyoming and was active in the Women's Suffrage Movement, working with Carrie Chapman Catt and Susan B. Anthony. She was also a civil engineer.

Born in Delta in 1894, Agnes Wright went through the local schools, showing a talent in both English and mathematics. After her high school days, her father moved to a ranch near Laramie, Wyoming, where he established a freight and stagecoach line between that city and coal mining towns.

At the University of Wyoming, Agnes became the first editor of a student newspaper and was the first woman to be enrolled in the engineering school. There she was given the nickname of "Old Ironsides" when the metal staves of her corset disturbed the compass needle used in surveying.

Agnes graduated as a civil engineer in 1913 but took a job in the library of the Wyoming Supreme Court until she was awarded a scholarship to Columbia University's Pulitzer School of Journalism. It was there that she became excited about the women's suffrage movement and first met the famous leaders, Carrie Chapman Catt and Susan B. Anthony.

After graduating with a master's degree, she rose up in indignation when offered a reporter's job at a leading New York City newspaper for only half the amount of pay given to men in the same position. She then returned to Wyoming where she took a position as the State Historian in Cheyenne.

In 1921, Agnes married geologist Archer Spring and spent several years traveling the West with him, interviewing old-timers for historical interest. They bought a cherry orchard at Fort Collins a few years later, and it was there that she wrote her first history, *Caspar Collins: The Life and Exploits of an Indian Fighter of the Sixties.* This was followed by twenty other books, more than 600 articles and fiction stories, and a play. She also edited the *Wyoming Stockman-Farmer* for more than a quarter century.

During World War II, Agnes became the Colorado State Historian, the only person to have served in that position for more than one state. She achieved national recognition for her outstanding service in the development of historical resources.

At the time of her death in 1988, she was working on a book recounting her efforts to promote women's rights in the United States.

ANNALS OF DELTA COUNTY

The Contributions of Muriel Marshall

Muriel Marshall finished her last book at the age of ninety, only months before losing her long battle with cancer in March of 2000. She wrote more about the history, landforms, and people of Delta County than anyone else, and she took myriad photographs to accompany her accounts.

Born in 1909 in New Mexico, Muriel and her husband Walter arrived at Austin in 1947. She had already written a successful historical novel about Ireland, although she had never lived there. She became feature editor of the *Delta Independent* and wandered high and low all over Delta and Mesa Counties — from the plateaus to the deepest valleys, and knew almost every ranch in the region.

Her books were accurate, but laced with a good sense of humor and irony: *Uncompahgre: A Guide to the Uncompahgre Plateau; Red Hole in Time* about people who dwelt in such places as Escalante Canyon; and *Grand Mesa: Island in the Sky,* the most comprehensive study of that mountain—its geology, biology, and history. A significant study of Delta was titled *Where the Rivers Meet.* Her final book was *The Awesome 'Dobie Badlands* in which she told of interesting people and happenings in a God-forsaken terrain.

One reviewer wrote about her books: "If more factual books were written in this fun-to-read way, we wouldn't have to prod students into reading history; they'd be reaching for it." She may not be with us, but Muriel Marshall will be telling us stories for many, many years to come — true stories of how things were in the first century after the Utes left.

INSPIRATION FOR
"LILIES OF THE FIELD?"

Driggs Mansion in Unaweep Canyon

Denver author William E. Barrett, who wrote *Lilies of the Field,* claimed that the inspiration for the famous novel and movie came from a vacation trip through Unaweep Canyon. It was there he saw what looked like an unfinished church, and the sight sparked the idea of immigrant Roman Catholic nuns building a church, helped by a black itinerant Protestant. The movie later won an Academy Award for Sidney Poitier.

The structure, which inspired this story, was, in fact, intended to be a forty room hunting lodge for E.M. Driggs of New York. Started in about 1917, it was built out of native stone, but probably only consisted of three of four rooms. Researchers James and Christine Keener interviewed nearby residents and wrote that Driggs had joined the military in World War I and was wounded badly, preventing his return.

The property was sold and used for a time as a hunting lodge. The ravages of time and vandalism eventually left very little of the structure standing, but the graceful archway entrance was reminiscent of a church.

Military
Matters

UFOs OVER BOOKCLIFFS
IN WORLD WAR I

Hidden German Airfield?

It's a plane, it's a bird—what is it? An alarm shook Grand Valley residents during World War I when unidentified objects were reportedly sighted over the Bookcliffs. The "air age" had just begun, and the only experience of "aeroplanes" in Grand Junction had been daring pilots performing at the fairgrounds (now Lincoln Park).

Skeptics thought they might have been sandhill cranes on their annual migration between New Mexico and Idaho, and were misidentified by war-hysterical viewers. After all, why would the Germans build an air base somewhere north of the Bookcliffs? The response was that they planned to bomb the railroad or the new roller dam in DeBeque Canyon and was recorded as such in the *Daily Sentinel*. Some observers claimed they did not exactly look like airplanes—more like balloons or flying saucers.

There were also speculations that the Army Air Force base at Salt Lake City was staging secret training missions, but this was quite a long distance away for the airplanes of that time and their limited fuel supplies.

Whatever caused the alarm seemed to have disappeared when the war ended. It would not be until World War II when a few Japanese incendiary balloons reached western Colorado and fell to earth, one near Collbran and another in Delta County, that the UFOs could be identified.

PARANOIA IN WORLD WAR I

Tar and Feathers in Appleton

In 1917, President Woodrow Wilson called what we now know as World War I, "The War to End All Wars." Throughout the United States, people with German names, many of them fourth generation Americans, were shunned and treated as enemies and spies. Western Colorado was no exception.

At Paonia, German Mesa was settled mostly by immigrants from that country, and the local newspaper editor demanded that the name be changed. It has been called Lamborn Mesa since then, although German Creek still runs through it.

Soon after the United States declared war, a young boy, west of Delta, went on an errand to a farmhouse, where he witnessed a meeting of three German families. The lad heard them discussing a water well, and, in a panic, he ran back to Delta and told people that the Germans were going to poison the town's water supply. Several men armed themselves and marched up to invade the meeting. Luckily one of the men asked about the conversation before taking action, and it turned out that the families were merely worrying about a common well of theirs, which had become polluted. The patriotic vigilantes sheepishly returned to town.

Gary Burke, Delta historian and teacher, found the following two articles in the *Delta County Independent* issue of April 19, 1918:

> ### TEACHING OF GERMAN ABOLISHED
> ### FROM DELTA SCHOOLS
> *The study of the German language has been banished from the high school of this city. This action was taken by teachers with consent of the board of education, and is in harmony with actions taken by high schools all over the country. It has long been evident that the continuance of the use of*

German language in our schools, churches and other insti-
tutions is not conducive to that spirit of loyalty to our coun-
try and to our allies that is needed at the present time.
Furthermore, after the war is over, German will not be a
popular language and there will be little occasion for its use.
Our high school authorities are to be congratulated on the
steps taken and, it is needless to say, these steps meet with
universal approval of the patriotic people of Delta.

Even more alarming was the second article in that same issue:

GRAND VALLEY INSTRUCTOR IS HUMILIATED –
TAR – FEATHERS
Dr. E. E. Cole, principal of the Appleton schools, eight
miles west of Grand Junction, was called from his home at
night by three masked men, stripped and decked with a
coat of tar and feathers. It was stated he had made pro-
German statements to his pupils.

Cole claims that he was teaching the textbook histo-
ry and had no thought of pro-Germanism. He was ordered
to leave or be hanged, but has announced his intention to
remain and defy his accusers. It is said that he has many
warm friends who are incensed at the treatment.

Years later people felt remorse over the often vicious treatment of German-Americans, and when America took part in World
War II, there was little anti-German hysteria. However, the Japanese-
Americans suffered similar and even more extreme discrimination
during that war.

THE FIRST DRAFTEE TO BECOME A FOUR-STAR GENERAL

Achievements of
Robert E. "Dutch" Huyser

Robert "Dutch" Huyser was born in 1924, one of five children of Bill and Alma Huyser, who had a farm on Matthews Lane west of Paonia. He attended grade school at Stewart Mesa, went to Paonia High School, graduating in 1942, and was drafted into the U.S. Army.

Assigned to what was then the Army Air Force, Dutch became an aviation cadet, flying B-24s and B-29s on combat missions as a commissioned "shavetail" Second Lieutenant. From then on, his career moved into high gear as he demonstrated outstanding leadership ability. He felt he had come a long way from what he called a "redheaded freckle-faced boy from Paonia."

General Robert Huyser
Courtesy of the *Daily Sentinel*,
Sept. 27, 1987

Consistent promotions led to Dutch becoming Chief of Combat Operations for the Far East Bomber Command in the Korean Conflict. By 1969, he was promoted to Brigadier General and Chief of Command Control at the Strategic Air Command. His work in developing strategic nuclear war plans for all U.S. forces brought another promotion, and he was moved into the Pentagon as director of plans and operations for the Air Force.

By 1975, Dutch Huyser was made a four-star general, the highest rank that can be obtained in peacetime, and became the first draftee in American history to have reached that rank. He served as commander-in-chief of the U.S. European Command, and later commander-in-chief of the Military Air Lift Command.

In 1979, President Carter sent him on a secret mission to Iran to find out if the Shah's threatened regime could be saved, or whether a successor should be endorsed by the United States. As Dutch predicted, the Ayatollah Khomeini gained control, resulting in the capture of the U.S. Embassy and the ensuing hostage crisis. Dutch's book on that subject, *Mission to Tehran,* is one of the most significant explanations of the entire tragic affair.

Dutch officially retired in 1981 but continued to work with youth groups, as a lecturer, and as a consultant for Boeing Aircraft Corporation. Each year the prestigious General Robert "Dutch" Huyser Award, popularly called "The Huyser," is given to a pilot, a flight engineer, a navigator, and a boom operator in the Air Force for outstanding performance.

The Western Colorado Air Force Association also named its chapter for him.

When once asked the reason for his success, he referred to his father, Billy, who had come from Holland in 1903 and who taught his children, "For every dollar paid, do two dollars worth of work." General Dutch Huyser died in 1987 and was buried at Arlington National Cemetery with full honors.

MEETING THE TROOPS
IN WORLD WAR II

Grand Junction's Train Stop Canteen

Grand Junction, like almost all towns in the nation, had many volunteer programs to help in the war effort during World War II. There were collection points for scrap paper, rubber, various metals, and a "Victory Book Drive" in which citizens donated books for service men and women. In a total break from her strict discipline, one lady algebra teacher announced that, for the duration of the war, students could use both sides of each sheet of paper for their assignments.

The local Red Cross was very active, and, since almost every troop train had to stop in Grand Junction for at least an hour of servicing, a troop canteen was set up at the railroad depot. Although troop movements were not made public, the leaders of the canteen were told when to be ready. At any hour of the day or night, when a troop train came in, there were volunteers to greet the servicemen when they were allowed off the train for a stretch.

They were given gifts donated for the purpose: stationary, post cards, postage stamps, candy, chewing gum, cigarettes, cigars, pipe tobacco, and even chewing tobacco. Cold soft drinks and often home-baked cookies were provided. During one September stop of 1942, local growers gave away 103 bushels of top grade Palisade peaches.

To keep the supplies up, there were donation spots all over the Grand Valley, and many merchants contributed merchandise to the cause. The American Legion Auxiliary and the Western Colorado Commercial Travelers' Association held campaigns to collect the contributions, which also included personal items such as toothbrushes and razor blades. Grand Junction's *Daily Sentinel* supplied the daily newspapers for all.

Volunteers from all over the valley would get out of bed, even at such outrageous hours as two or four o'clock in the morning, to greet the soldiers, sailors, marines, or coast guards at the station. Estelle Brumbaugh, chairman of the canteen service, coordinated the effort. She would also speak to service clubs and church groups about the "Treat for the Troops" campaign. Several soldiers or sailors wrote notes of appreciation to the local Red Cross, and one even stated that this was the only place during their whole trip where they had received such a reception.

P.O.W. ESCAPE!

Foiled in Ruby Canyon, Saved By a Mirror

During World War II, several prisoner-of-war camps were established to help the farm harvests in the Grand Valley. One of these was set up for German prisoners near the west entrance to Colorado National Monument, south of Fruita.

One prisoner must have known enough geography to realize that the Colorado River near the camp flowed into the Gulf of California in Mexico. He and a friend simply walked away from the harvesting work, reached the river, and followed it to their intended freedom. However, having no concept of the distance involved, they thought the river would flow through rich farmlands so that they could live off the land and steal from farms and food storage cellars. When they reached the first of the deep desert canyons, Ruby Canyon, the two began to wonder about the viability of their plan. They climbed a cliff, and, feeling hungry, decided it might be time to reconsider.

The problem about returning to the camp was that in their prison clothes they might be shot on sight. So they waited for nightfall and made their way to U.S. Highway 6 near Mack. There they slept in a haystack on the north side of the highway. The next day became even more frightening as there were several farms to cross in order to get back to the camp.

One of the men had a small mirror. They noticed a Highway Patrol car as it drove along the road to the Utah border. After several failed attempts, they were able to reflect the sun at the car enough to attract the trooper's attention. When he stopped, they ran forth with hands up and were returned to the safety of the camp, their understanding of western American geography much improved.

THE MEMORIAL BELL TOWER

Built by Mesa College Students

The bell tower on the campus of Mesa State College is possibly the only structure on a Colorado state college campus that was designed, voluntarily financed, and physically constructed entirely

Memorial Bell Tower built by Mesa Junior College students.

Photo by Randy Fay

by students. It is a memorial to forty-two former students of Mesa Junior College who were killed in World War II, and a plaque includes their names.

After World War II, the U.S. Navy gave the college a bell from a Navy ship. For several years, it was used to celebrate athletic victories. In 1964, the students decided it should have a permanent structure.

Pre-engineering and art students designed the project, which was approved by the college architect. Students who knew how to lay bricks and make concrete forms volunteered their labor.

Various clubs and organizations on the campus raised financial donations for the tower. It took several months before the monument was completed and the bell suspended.

Because occasional miscreants sometimes rang the bell at night, disturbing neighbors near the campus, a college official removed the clapper, and it disappeared forever. Still the tower stands as a solemn tribute to the memory of those who died in defense of the nation, and a reminder of student initiative and determination years later.

Delights for Eyes, Ears and Tongues

GLORY DAYS IN THE
PARK OPERA HOUSE

And A Death on the Stage

The great Park Opera House once stood at what is now the parking lot of the Museum of Western Colorado on Ute Avenue. Opened in June of 1891, it was second only to Aspen's Wheeler Opera House in western Colorado, in terms of cost. However, the *Grand Junction News* pointed out that "with all due respect to Aspen, [the Wheeler] is far inferior to ours in beauty and the thoroughness of equipment."

The Park was a three-story building complete with a parquet, dress circle, balcony, and gallery. It cost $25,000 — an enormous sum in those days. There were multiple dressing rooms for performers and a large stage. "Retirement rooms" were available for both ladies and gentlemen of the audience. Performances were almost

The Park Opera House was in use from the 1890s until the 1920s when moving pictures changed theatrical demands.

Mrs. Walter J. Eames Collection, Loyd Files Research Library, Museum of Western Colorado, 1983.2.

every evening during the first decades of the theater. Professional talent was featured in operas, in plays by Shakespeare and George Bernard Shaw, and various minstrel shows.

Probably the most dramatic occurrence on any Grand Junction stage took place at the Park on February 18, 1892. A famous elderly actor, Hal Newton Carlyle, dropped dead while performing on stage, perhaps due to either a massive stroke or heart attack.

As his widow and son were at home in New York City, time and costs dictated that Carlyle be given a funeral and buried at what was then Fairmont Cemetery "to await the Dawn of the Never-Ending Day." The local Bannister Undertakers were retained by Carlyle's New York manager, and both the Knights of Pythias and the Masons took part in the ceremonies, held Sunday, February 23rd.

One of the most popular entertainers at the Park was child star Buster Brown with his trick dog, Tyge. Sponsored by the shoe manufacturer (still in business), Buster Brown fell in love with western Colorado and, later as an adult, bought a ranch near Craig, where he died in 1976 at the age of seventy-seven.

Buster Brown performed at Park Opera House.
Courtesy of the Buster Brown Corporation

When the even more impressive Avalon Theater was built in the 1920s, the Park had already deteriorated due to neglect and was no longer of much use. C.D. Smith Hardware then built its huge warehouse next door and finally had the building torn down. The warehouse now houses the Museum of Western Colorado.

"THE DEAN OF COLORADO CAMERAMEN"

"Fotografer" Frank Dean

An edition of *Who's Who in American Portrait Photography* designated Frank E. Dean of Grand Junction "the acknowledged dean of Colorado cameramen." His landscape photos of western Colorado won national and international prizes.

Frank E. Dean.
Courtesy of Molly Dean Stucker

Frank Dean was born in Marshalltown, Iowa, in 1864, and his family moved to Sedalia, Missouri, five years later. At the age of ten he was already working for a local photographer and learning the art. In 1882, eighteen-year-old Frank arrived in Gunnison, Colorado, and opened his own studio. Two years later he married Lucy Buckey from Wisconsin. His photography was so much in demand that he opened additional studios in Crested Butte and Lake City.

Moving to Grand Junction in 1900, his first studio was a tent on the southwest corner of 5th Street and Rood Avenue. It was there he built a permanent building for his studio and an upstairs dance hall featuring live bands. A huge sign read "Fotografer," which became his unique trademark, attracting and amusing many customers. Soon he was able to build a home next door for his family — Lucy, three daughters, and one son.

While his early photos of local people and scenes of the town have become classics, it was his spectacular shots of such scenes as Colorado National Monument and "Miracle Rock," the huge balanced stone near Glade Park, that were celebrated in national and international photography shows. He also served as President of the Intermountain Association of Photographers.

Frank was active in many local organizations, and Lucy was a leader in the Catholic Church and Red Cross. She died in 1938. Two years later, in 1940, Frank married Sarah Walsh. She died in 1946. Frank Dean continued to take photographs until his own death in 1947.

Frank Dean's famous photo of Cold Shivers Point, Colorado National Monument.
Courtesy of Molly Dean Stucker

A SHY BUT FAMOUS ARTIST

Harold Bryant's View of the West

Very shy and often grouchy, Harold Bryant was perhaps the greatest painter to depict the American West of the early Twentieth Century as Frederick Remington and Charles Russell had in the earlier "Wild West" days. Born in Nebraska in 1894, Harold's father, a Dunker minister and farmer, purchased a farm at Appleton, a suburb of Grand Junction, in 1903. Early on, Harold showed a remarkable talent for authentic sketches of horses and cattle. Graduating from Appleton High School in 1914, he went to Chicago and eked out his education at the Art Institute by taking numerous odd jobs, including dishwashing and janitorial positions. In time, he was able to get several low-paying commercial art assignments and he began to attract attention with the authentic detail of his work.

He returned to the Grand Valley in 1917 and enlisted in the Army for service in World War I. Harold loved music, learning to play a violin and a trumpet, and was appointed saxophone player for an Army band that toured the West before being sent to England and France. His unit went to the front lines, and he suffered gas poisoning. Following the war, while his band toured the great cities of Europe, he viewed some of the great artists' works before being sent back home in 1919.

Bryant returned to Chicago, where he continued to produce artwork for advertising agencies and illustrations for western novels. He later had a studio in New York City, where the Grand Central Gallery displayed his western oil paintings — his real love. He had invested his money in the stock market, and when the crash of 1929 occurred, Harold lost almost all his savings.

He returned to Appleton to help with the farm and retreated to a cabin he had bought on Piñon Mesa to meditate, paint, and shut the world out during the Great Depression. Harold became almost a hermit. Later, he tried to make it again in New York City, nearly starving because art had become less popular as an investment and advertising neglected western themes.

In 1938, Ruth, a lady from Brooklyn who had been with the Naval Intelligence Service during World War I, entered a bar and saw

Harold Bryant paintings owned by Ed Beckwith, Jr.

the sullen Bryant sitting in a corner. She asked the barkeeper about the "old grouch" and was informed he was an impoverished artist. Although a "confirmed bachelor," Bryant was charmed by Ruth when she approached him and asked about his stories of the West.

Nearly penniless, he headed for home once more, admitting to Ruth that he loved her. She threw away all other dreams and went to Denver, where Harold's married sister, Barbara, lived. Barbara and Ruth plotted to promote Bryant's works, but Harold would have none of it. He refused to show his works, as he would be expected to appear in person, meet strangers, and, most horrible perhaps, to give a talk. He spent more time than ever in his lonely cabin.

After a long battle with illness at Fitzsimmons Hospital in Denver, Ruth came over the Divide to marry Harold. He was practically dragged to the Justice of the Peace in Grand Junction in 1940 to be married, and they started housekeeping in his cabin. When Harold's father died, they had to move down to take over the farm. Ruth still kept campaigning for Harold's art, success coming at last when several magazines such as *Atlantic Monthly, Capper's Farmer,* and even *Fortune* featured his paintings. Several companies issued calendars with his work, so gradually his cowboys, Indians, horses, and cows were displayed in thousands of homes. There was a real demand for the originals, especially in Texas.

Seagrams' Whiskey issued posters of Bryant's paintings, which decorated bars throughout the United States and Canada. Texaco featured his works in advertisements. His paintings were used on the covers of sports magazines, and there was a renewed demand for book illustrations and dust jackets.

In his small Appleton studio, he was reluctant to greet visitors, and buyers still considered him a bit of a grouch despite his nationwide success. He would go on many lonely trips throughout the West and come back with new ideas. By 1949, he had painted eighty-five canvases and several hundred of his illustrations. It was then that he came down with what was thought to be "tick fever," but was diagnosed as cancer. He died at the Grand Junction Veterans' Hospital on January 19, 1950.

Ruth lived on until 1973. She owned quite a number of Harold's paintings and hoped Grand Junction would build a museum to house his works. When there seemed to be little interest in Colorado, but much interest in Texas, the collection was given to the Texas Technological University at Lubbock, which now houses the largest collection of his paintings and sketches. The Western Colorado Center for the Arts has the second largest collection and displays Bryant's works on a rotating basis. There are also some private owners in the Grand Junction area.

In 1961, Al Look published a biography, *Harold Bryant, Maverick With a Paint Brush,* which contains forty-nine prints of his works. It is still available in several local libraries.

THE LADY WITH THE CAMERA

Ola's DeBeque Studio

Born in Iowa in 1874, Ola Anfenson was the daughter of a Swedish minister. She learned photography while working as a retoucher in a San Francisco studio.

Visiting her sister in Grand Junction, Ola stayed on for a while and worked for the pioneer photographer Frank Dean. After other travels and adventures in California, she returned to Grand Junction to be near her parents, who had moved there because of poor health. She lived in a small house at 820 North Avenue.

When her father died, Ola and her mother moved to DeBeque, where Ola established her own studio. This is believed to have been the only photography studio owned and operated by a woman in Colorado in the early years of the Twentieth Century. Her photographs of local people, ranchers, and businesses were outstanding in quality. She also photographed the first gas and oil well in that region, a gusher in 1912. It caught fire, and she took pictures of the flaming plume both by day and by night.

In 1914, she fell in love with another photographer, Fred Garrison of Rifle. When they married, Ola also became his business partner, moving with her mother to Rifle. She spent the rest of her career there and later moved with her husband to Canada. She died in 1970 at the age of ninety-six. Her glass photography plates were donated to the Colorado Historical Society. A book containing some of her works, written by Natasha Boyd, a friend of Ola's, was published in 1997 by Horizon Communications of Albuquerque, New Mexico.

BIGGEST CROWD FOR A PERFORMANCE IN GRAND JUNCTION?

The Morning After Eugene Debs Showed Up, Too

Labor Day of 1908 may have witnessed the biggest gate attendance for any performance in Grand Junction history when Buffalo Bill's Wild West Show and Congress of Rough Riders of the World came to town.

William F. Cody's show had established a reputation throughout the United States and Europe since it first opened in 1882. It was a feature of the World Columbian Exposition in Chicago in 1893 and had performed in the major cities of twelve European countries. It sometimes had as many as 500 horses. Sharp shooter Annie Oakley was a star performer along with Sioux Chief Sitting Bull himself.

Grand Junction, midway between Denver and Salt Lake City, attracted quite a few remarkable shows because of the necessary maintenance stop on the railroad trips. At that time, the entire population of Mesa County numbered less than 10,000, so it was amazing that the reported gate attendance totaled more than 10,000. Special trains came from Ouray, Montrose, Delta, Glenwood Springs, and intermediate stops carrying people to see the extravaganza.

The night before the Wild West Show appeared, Socialist presidential candidate, Eugene V. Debs, had drawn a crowd of over 5,000, certainly one of the biggest audiences for a political speaker. He brought with him the Chicago Volunteer Socialist Band and appealed to many depression-weary citizens with his ideas of reform. After Debs' train left, people waited around in the early hours for the arrival of the three Wild West Show trains, fifty-seven cars in all. Bleachers to hold the huge crowd were erected at the edge

179

of town at Pitkin Avenue and 9th Street. By 11a.m. the show began, and by 2 p.m. it packed up to depart for Salt Lake City.

The audience enjoyed acts from all over the world in those three hours. Of course, Buffalo Bill himself, at age sixty-two, was the star attraction. In succeeding years poor management and bad investments brought the demise of the show and finally Buffalo Bill had to join the Sells-Floto Circus, founded by Harry Tammen, publisher of the *Denver Post*. Buffalo Bill lost his huge ranch near North Platte, Nebraska, and most of his property in Cody, Wyoming, the town he founded.

Buffalo Bill's last performance was in November of 1916. Two months later, he died in Denver. The *Denver Post* staged the funeral and burial on Lookout Mountain despite his wish to be interred at Cody. A huge block of concrete was placed over the casket to prevent people from Wyoming from raiding the grave and taking Bill to his intended resting place.

THE SAVAGE BELLS IN DELTA

And the Man Who Collected Them

When Leslie J. Savage was in elementary school at Hamburg, Arkansas, his teacher gave him a school bell. That was his first in a lifetime hobby of collecting bells. Most of those bells now hang on the grounds of the Delta County Historical Museum, a small part of his legacy in western Colorado.

Born in 1883, Leslie never had a formal education beyond the fifth grade, but became a bank president and served on the Board of Trustees of the State Colleges of Colorado for twenty-nine years. In 1906, he married Sallie Lucile Noble, and they had three daughters. In 1910, he was stricken with tuberculosis and went to a sanitarium in New Mexico. Believing he had recovered, he took a position working in a bank at Fountain Hill, Arkansas.

Leslie Savage Bells. Delta County Historical Society Museum

Then the dreaded disease reappeared and his employer, E.W. Gates, who owned some ranches near Crawford, Colorado, hired Leslie for the position of ranch bookkeeper at twenty-five dollars per month. Leslie took up a homestead near Crawford and gradually the high, dry, and sunny climate overcame his illness. At first the family lived in a tent, but then moved to Hotchkiss, where the girls could go to school. In 1918 Crawford opened a school so they moved into the home that he would occupy for the rest of his life.

He kept books for Gates until 1920 and secured a position in the local bank. In the yard of his Crawford home, he erected a scaffold on which to hang the bells he acquired—school bells, church bells, ships' bells, and ranch bells.

Over the years, he became president of the bank. His interest in Western State College in Gunnison involved him in politics, and, in 1935, he was appointed as Trustee to the State Colleges of Colorado. Leslie also spearheaded a long campaign, which eventually led to the widening and paving of the spectacular dirt road from Hotchkiss to Sapinero, en route to Gunnison along the Black Canyon.

During the years of the Great Depression of the 1930s, Leslie was able to keep the Crawford Bank solvent despite the bankruptcies of his clients. When he finally closed the bank in 1941, all depositors were paid in full.

When the New Deal was providing Public Works Administration funds for the other college building projects, Leslie became irate that Western State College was overlooked. He took it upon himself to lead a campaign all the way to Washington, and was successful in getting federal support for the college. This resulted in several Spanish style buildings and the beautiful library, which was named in his honor. Years later, when the library was expanded, Savage donated a carillon to the library.

Always a promoter, Leslie was active in the Chamber of Commerce in Delta and Grand Junction, the North Fork Conservancy District, and the board of directors for the Delta County Hospital. Leslie Savage finally retired from the Western State Trustees in 1964 due to poor eyesight and hearing. He died in 1969.

THE KING OF SIAM'S ROBE IN DELTA

A Result of the McCarty Bank Robbery

In 1854, England established an agreement with King Mongkut in Siam to allow British citizens to live and own land in that country. Mongkut employed Dr. Don Beach Bradley as his personal physician and Mary Bradley, the doctor's wife, as governess for his children. The Bradleys had a great influence on Mongkut, introducing him to some of the wonders of the Western World. They had several children, among them Mary Adelle, who was born on the royal grounds of Bangkok and lived there nineteen years.

Mrs. Bradley retired from teaching in 1862 in order to care for her children. Her successor was Anna Leonowens, a Welsh lady who had children of her own. Anna wrote two books about life in the Royal Court of Bangkok, and these later became the basis for the book *Anna and the King of Siam*. This in turn became the subject of the famous musical, *The King and I*, and a later movie, *Anna and the King*.

Dr. Bradley served for a long time, and was awarded a Royal Peace Medal. His

King of Siam's Robe, Delta County Historical Society Museum.
Courtesy of the Delta County Historical Society

family was given two ivory toys and one of the King's royal robes, made of black silk with silver embroidery, as gifts of appreciation. Mary Adelle Bradley inherited the gifts from the King of Siam and, after her marriage to Trew Blachly, eventually moved to Delta. Blachly became the owner of the Farmers and Merchants Bank of Delta and was shot and killed by the infamous McCarty gang in a hold-up in 1893.

Trew's death left Mary a widowed mother of eight sons, so she taught music lessons and did other work to see all of the boys through school. The King's robe, medal, and toys eventually fell into the possession of Margaret Bradley Visardi, Mary's descendent and schoolteacher in Meeker, Colorado. She donated them to the Delta County Historical Society Museum, where they are beautifully displayed as a tribute to Mary Blachly.

ACCEPTING ONLY THE
FINEST SCULPTORS

Land's End Foundry at Paonia

Bob and Mary Zimmerman's achievements became so much in demand that they left Loveland, Colorado, and moved to Paonia. Their skill in producing the bronze renditions of artists' wood or clay sculpture had brought more assignments than they could handle. At one point as many as 600 artists wanted to cast their works with them.

They established the Land's End Foundry and limited their clientele to only about fifty of the nation's finest sculptors. At least one, Lincoln Fox, became so enamored with the region that he bought property nearby and established his home and studio there. Others flew in from regions as far away as New England to help polish off the final castings of their statuary.

It was in Paonia that the largest wildlife sculpture in existence was made. The sculpture depicts a group of thirty-two-foot-tall sailfish and is displayed in a town center at Fort Lauderdale, Florida. A huge cowboy sculpture cast at Paonia stands in Denver's 16th Street Mall. A group of horse statues were shipped for display at the Houston Astrodome in Texas. An eighteen-foot "Casey at the Bat" may be viewed in South Carolina.

Noted Maine sculptor Toby Hart preferred Land's End for his exclusive works. The Zimmermans are both sculptors, and some of their works have been displayed in Grand Junction's downtown section, the largest collection of outdoor statuary in Colorado.

WEDDLE'S GARDENS

From Petunias of Paonia to Prickly Pears of Palisade

A native of Texas, Charles L. Weddle moved to Paonia in 1947 to grow better petunias. Thus was established what became Pan American Gardens, Inc.

Chosen because of its strong light and clear air, the garden site soon became a spectacular kaleidoscope of color. By 1958, Weddle's special breeding of petunias earned him the highest honor that can be received by the American Seed Trade Association. He became known around the nation as "Mister Petunia."

Cultivation of the seeds was a painstaking process in greenhouses carefully guarded for light, humidity, and temperature. A main precaution was protection against accidental pollination by insects. The mature plants were then set out in specified rows. By July, visitors were allowed to tour the acres of blooming petunias and other flowers.

Charles also spent ten years improving the snapdragon, eventually developing a new generation seed that became the elite of that species. He then went to work on the hollyhock, and it was in Paonia that the original "double hollyhocks" were bred.

Pan American was generous to local gardeners, sharing many of the plants. Soon, tourists began coming to the town just to look at the gardens. Filling stations, churches, and planters along Grand Avenue all displayed petunias long before the concept of growing flowers in business districts became popular. After all, Paonia was named for a flower — the peony.

In the early 1970s, Pan American merged with the huge Ball Seed Company of Chicago. Charles continued his work on the flowers, but eventually realized that the larger company was dominating the policies of germination. He then moved to Palisade and began another unique form of cultivation — native plants. Ball later abandoned the Paonia gardens, although the name Pan American Seeds was still used elsewhere.

At Palisade, Weddle introduced systematic xeriscapy, the decorative use of native desert plants, which require little water to grow. While there had been some individual experimenters of this landscaping technique in the Grand Valley, the new nursery demonstrated the practical applications and called attention to the beauty of xeriscapy.

Gradually lawns disappeared and were replaced with a new showing of desert beauty. Weddle introduced some new types of yucca, prickly pear cactus, varied forms of other cacti, and bushes, which thrived with little or no water. He also promoted the use of beautiful rocks and tastefully placed borders to enhance the effects.

With the reality of drought conditions and demands on water by a growing population, his ideas may eventually become far more prevalent than former concepts of gardening. Charles Weddle continued to cultivate his gardens almost to the time of his passing in February of 1987. He left a legacy of beauty in both Paonia and Palisade.

OBSERVING THE EQUINOX

The Unique Sculpture

Thousands of people walk by a rather large skeleton-like sculpture on the Mesa State College campus without realizing its astronomical significance. Located on the academic quad walkway, it has special importance two days a year: on the vernal equinox and the autumnal equinox. If the sun is shining on the morning of the vernal equinox, the shadow of the pattern of the structure will fall into place on a visible marking on Wubben Hall, directly behind it. In the afternoon of the first day of autumn, the shadows fall on markings in the grass to the north of the structure. That's why the sculptor, student William C. Burgess, named it "AM/PM."

Equinox Sculpture. Mesa State College

THE SWEET TASTE OF SUCCESS

World-Famous Almond Toffee

On the last voyage of the famous ocean liner, the Queen Elizabeth, those at the captain's table were served Enstrom's almond toffee. The candy has been carried up to the summit of Mount Everest at least two times to celebrate victorious climbs. Royalty from around the world are said to praise the confection made in Grand Junction.

As a high school student in Colorado Springs, Chester (Chet) Enstrom worked weekends and summers for an ice cream company.

Chet and Vernie Enstrom — late 1960s.
Courtesy of Enstrom Candies

189

After graduation, he got a full-time job with Barthol's Confectionary, which made both ice cream and candies. While he was soon made manager of the ice cream manufacture and sales, during the winter, when that treat was in less demand, Chet helped make candy and thereby found his life's ambition.

A Greek salesman gave Chet the recipe for almond toffee, including a requirement that the ingredients must be mixed with a wooden paddle and cooled on a marble slab.

In 1929, Chet married a woman named Vernie and moved with her to Grand Junction. With a partner, they opened the Jones-Enstrom Ice Cream Company, producing Velvet ice cream. One of the most popular flavors of that brand was toffee.

At home, Chet experimented in his basement kitchen with the almond toffee. It required some detailed control—too hot and it would scorch; too cold and the ingredients would separate. He and Vernie started giving the candy to family and friends, who loved it. The preservation of the toffee was delicate—no direct sunlight, and special storage boxes to minimize breakage.

In 1960, the Enstroms sold the ice cream business and began making candy full time in their store at Seventh Street and Ute Avenue. Their confection candies were all popular, but the toffee led the sales. Special equipment was invented — special heating timers and water-cooled tables — to keep the product quality with larger production.

By 1965, 10,000 pounds of almond toffee were sold both locally and to 750 mail-order customers in fifty countries. Chet and Vernie turned the business over to their son, Emit, and his wife, May, when Chet was appointed to a vacancy in the Colorado Senate. It has remained in the family ever since.

As of this writing Enstrom Candies produces over a half-million pounds of almond toffee per year. There are retail stores in Grand Junction, Aspen, and Denver, but eighty-five per cent of the candy is shipped out by mail order.

A Few More Characters and Oddities

THE REMARKABLE
"MOCCASIN BILL"

*He Killed a Bear with a
Shotgun Shell*

A gravestone in the cemetery at Crawford, Colorado, marks the final resting place of one of Colorado's great outdoorsmen of the Old West, William H. Perkins. According to his mother, Bill Perkins was born in Indianapolis, Indiana, in 1823 with six teeth already in place. He grew into a muscular six-foot-four-inch frame, weighing in at about 200 pounds.

Not much is known of his early life, but he served as a scout in the Civil War when he was about forty years old. After that, he came west to the Rocky Mountains to try mining and big game hunting. Bill located a claim above timberline near the town of Rosita, in the Wet Mountain Valley just east of the Sangre de Cristo Mountains.

During the winter of 1868, he and his helpers ran short of provisions. While Bill stayed on to work in the mine, the others went down into town to get some more supplies. Apparently they imbibed whiskey to the point that they forgot their mission. After they had sobered up, they discovered that a huge snowfall had wiped out the trail to the mine.

Growing very hungry, Bill used the few remaining supplies and kept boiling the coffee "till it wouldn't even color the snow." At last, he was forced to make the trek through the deep snows to find food at Rosita. He had only moccasins on his feet, and they froze before he was able to finish the painful hike. His feet were so terribly frozen, in fact, that he could not remove the moccasins without stripping the flesh from the soles. In order to hobble along, he put on a larger pair of moccasins. As his feet continued to swell, he repeated that process until it appeared he had enormous feet. That was when people began calling him "Moccasin Bill." Even after he was able to shed his footwear, he was called that for the rest of his life.

When silver was discovered at Leadville, Perkins went there to make his fortune. He was not successful but did succeed in hunting bear, deer, and elk, which were in demand in the mining camp. He spent many years wandering the mountains as a hunter, going from place to place and camping wherever he and his burro found themselves. Later, he settled for the winters at the town of Crawford. Among his other talents, Bill played the violin and was a popular fiddler for North Fork country get-togethers.

One day while hunting in the West Elk Range, Moccasin Bill was carrying a double-barreled weapon, one barrel loaded with fine birdshot and the other bored for regular rifle ammunition. Suddenly he came upon a grizzly bear cub, hastily took aim, and shot at the creature. The rifle bullet passed through the cub and hit its mother, who was just out of sight behind the bush.

The angry bear attacked at once, but Bill was able to sidestep the onslaught just enough to grab hold of a small tree, which he climbed as quickly as he could.

Bent on revenge, the bear also began to climb the tree, opening her jaws to grab his foot. Bill shoved his shotgun barrel down her throat and pulled the trigger. The wounded bear began bleeding from the mouth and wandered away. Two days later, Perkins found her body nearby. That may be the only case in which a bear was killed by a shotgun.

At the age of eighty, Moccasin Bill still had great eyesight and his accuracy with a rifle was well known. He continued hunting in the mountains by himself and usually returned with game. According to his own records, he killed a total of 149 bears during his career. He fathered four boys, each of whom died before him, and six daughters, all of whom survived him when he died on November 18, 1904, at the age of eighty-two.

THE HOLY POACHER

First Game Laws in the Plateau Valley

In the first few years after the Plateau Valley was settled in 1882, people depended on hunting in order to feed themselves. By 1885, so much wildlife had been slaughtered that the region established game restrictions. These included a ban on killing deer or elk until the herds would be replenished.

People were shocked when the first violator arrested was a local minister, Reverend Babb of Collbran, who collected only the hides and heads of the animals and would leave the meat for the ravens. Pioneer settler Alex Hawxhurst remembered that Reverend Babb was quoted as saying, "I have saved twenty souls, and calloused indeed is the human mind that would put the life of an animal above a human soul. Gentlemen, the end justifies the means and I shall continue." In spite of his plea, he was given a heavy fine.

There was so much killing of deer in those first decades that almost the entire population of Paonia turned out in 1906 to look at a rare deer that had wandered close to the town. In 1908, the Aspen Elks' Lodge imported a herd of elk from Wyoming to make up for the lack of natural population. Due to the hunting ban, that herd may well be the ancestry of most of the elk in western Colorado. It was not until after World War I that limited deer and elk hunting was again legalized.

THOSE GRAND MESA SKEETERS

They Take the Pot

Many a tale has been spun about the voracious mosquitoes of Grand Mesa. We thought we had heard them all until reading a book by the late Elmer Orr of Montrose, *Experience in Lieu of Education*. In it, Orr relates a fable regarding a camp cook with a construction crew on Grand Mesa, where they were building a dam. The cook had a big iron kettle. The mosquitoes were so huge and numerous that the cook climbed under the kettle to escape them. However, he found that they bored right through the kettle to reach him. The cook found a rock under there, and, when one mosquito stuck his beak through the kettle, the fugitive would clinch it with the rock. Finally, there were so many mosquitoes fastened to the kettle that they flew away with it, and the other mosquitoes came in a swarm and devoured the hapless cook.

HAUNTED BY GHOSTS
OF HIS VICTIMS

Killer Sam Angevine

Sam Angevine, a native of Nova Scotia, was one of the earliest settlers in the North Fork country. He served as a cowboy near Crawford and then homesteaded near Paonia. Angevine was known to have a very vicious temper. As a result of a fistfight where he was badly beaten, he bought a six-shooter and removed the trigger so that he could fire merely by releasing his thumb from the hammer. It was said that he was also quite paranoid and would never let anyone ride behind him.

During an argument with John McIntyre over a preemption claim, Sam pulled his pistol and wounded McIntyre seriously, claiming self-defense. Later, in an argument over a fish trap, he shot and killed Riley Adams. He escaped the law, and a thousand dollar reward was offered for his capture and return. He then went into hiding in the West Elk Mountains for a time, but then was tracked by a posse to Rawlins, Wyoming.

He was finally apprehended in Canada and was returned to Colorado. In the ensuing trial, he again claimed self-defense. A possibly intimidated jury found him not guilty. It is believed that Sam had killed other men earlier in his life. He became obsessed with the idea that the ghosts of his victims were haunting him, and that living men were out to get him. He would sweep his earthen floor in the cabin whenever he left for any reason, so he could detect tracks if anyone had come in. He never turned a light on at night for fear he'd be shot through one of the windows. If he had any suspicions that something was amiss, he would empty his sugar bowl or anything else he thought might be poisoned. He once shot at his own shadow. Gradually, his anguish was so great that he turned the triggerless weapon on himself.

THE SWASTIKA STONE

John Otto's Landmark for a New Era

Centuries before Adolf Hitler's Nazi Party adopted the swastika as its symbol, the design was used as a holy symbol both in ancient India and by American Indians, for whom it was a representation of good luck.

In 1915, John Otto, founder and first superintendent of the Colorado National Monument, was invited to San Francisco for the opening of Monument Park (Golden Gate) as part of the Pan American Exposition. He was very impressed by the ceremonies, and when he returned, his imaginative mind saw the event as the

Otto's Swastika Stone

beginning of a new era of prosperity and happiness for the United States. He had long heralded the idea of an "Ocean to Ocean Highway," which would come through Grand Junction and preferably over the Colorado National Monument.

For this reason, he obtained a huge block of granite and had it carved into a cubic form, with one side dominated by a huge swastika, which he called the "cross of the ages." On another side are the letters P.P.I.E., which stood for "Permanent Place for Inhabitants of the Earth." He rearranged the calendar for 1915 on the rock, designating March 1 (old count) as Year 1 (new count). This would be the "Golden Age which will begin at the Golden Gate." There are also initials carved: WW for World Welfare and THLF for Truth, Honor, Love, and Faith.

At the top of the stone, a hole was drilled for a pole to display the U.S. flag. The stone was placed at Sixth and Main Streets in Grand Junction but later was moved to South Broadway and Monument Road. During World War II, the swastika was whitewashed to conceal the hated symbol of Nazism.

As of this writing, the stone is located on the grounds of the Museum of Western Colorado, just north of the Whitman Educational building at Fourth and Ute Avenues.

This stone monument represented just one example of the sometimes strange thoughts of John Otto, who was committed briefly on three occasions to insane asylums. He not only founded Colorado National Monument, but created the Serpent's Trail Road leading up the east side of the Monument to the summit area. He also laid out the trail that would become the Land's End Road on Grand Mesa, and pioneered other trails in the region. When Otto decided to do something, he made it happen, one way or another.

WHEN THE GILMANS CAME TO TOWN IN DEBEQUE

She Shot, He Danced

Nearly a hundred years ago, Shake and Mattie Gilman had a ranch up Roan Creek above the town of DeBeque. Shake was well over six feet tall, and his wife, Mattie, by contrast, was quite tiny.

They would come to town every now and then to stock up on supplies and do a little drinking and gambling. Mattie was regarded as a shrewd poker player and a hard drinker. Sometimes after an afternoon spent consuming whiskey, Mattie would draw her pistol and chase Shake out onto the street, firing at his feet to make him dance. They both seemed to enjoy the game, and the townsfolk looked forward to the ritual. Shake always managed to dodge the bullets.

However, an "accident" occurred out on the ranch when Mattie shot and killed Shake, whom she had chased up a tree. It was assumed they were just playing their usual games, and Mattie was never charged.

Nearly everyone in the area showed up for Shake's funeral, which was held in the Odd Fellow's Hall, still a landmark in downtown DeBeque.

ACKNOWLEDGEMENTS

The author is indebted to a multitude of people who have supplied information for this book. These include the following library staffs and volunteers: Mesa County in Grand Junction, Palisade and Fruita; Delta and Paonia; Mesa State College; and the Lloyd Files Research Center at the Museum of Western Colorado. Historical organizations have been sources of many true stories: Mesa County and Delta County Historical Associations; Surface Creek in Cedaredge, North Fork in Paonia, and Hotchkiss-Crawford Associations; and the Lower Valley Heritage Group in Fruita.

Many individuals are owed thanks for making this work possible. These include,

From Grand Junction: Orville Boge, Steven Bradley, Ruth Edfast, Alfred Gofreddi, Pat Gormley, Anne Gould, Louie Herrera, Don Hobbs, Dale Hollingsworth, Marian Jacobson, Jim Kyle, John McConnel, Erin McIntyre, Marilyn McLaughlin, I.J. Nicholson, Frances Paiva, Dean Phillips, Judy Prosser-Armstrong, Mike Ruspil, Verdi Savage, Robert Smith, Molly Dean Stucker, Ruth Wayman, Daniel Weddle, Martin Wenger, Sissi Williams, Hazlet Wubben, and the Mesa State College Journal history staff members. From Palisade: Bill and Ed Beckwith, Bill and Lucille Floriancic, Lindon Granat, Al Merlino, Gary Granat, Harry Talbott, and Harold Vorhees. From Hotchkiss: John and Barbara Burrit, Ward Holder, Inez Pottorff, Tom Roberts and Jean Wigger; Paonians Alice Abseck, Shirley Lund, Jacque Koehler, Judy Livingston, and Margaret Wade; Gary Burke, Mildred Hamilton and Jim Wetzel in Delta; DeBeque's Karen Eisenach, B.J. Jaquelin, and Jim Rudnick. Yvonne Peterson and Tommy Pierce of Fruita offered good material, as did Ken Snyder of Cedaredge; In Crawford, Mamie Ferrier and Martha Savage; Gateway's Jean Moores; Alice Hubbard in Loma, Susan Corey and Jackie Lemerise of Collbran both contributed a great deal to this work (Jackie as Palisade Librarian.) Sue Chapman of Kannah Creek near Whitewater supplied information, as did David

A
C
K
N
O
W
L
E
D
G
E
M
E
N
T
S

Wetzel of Denver. Thanks also to photographer Frank Carr of Vienna, Virginia.

Production of the book itself owes much to Jan and P. David Smith, and Carole London of Montrose and Nancy Lewis-Lentz of Denver. Finally and very importantly, have been the untiring efforts of my wife, Joan, and family, Collin Fay, Marisa Fay, Dede Fay, Dave Batura, and Randy Fay.

BIBLIOGRAPHY
(All places are in Colorado unless marked otherwise.)

American Gilsonite Company. *Gilsonite Guide Book*, Salt Lake City, Utah, 1969.

Andreas, A.T. *Kansas Historical Collections*, Vol. 6, Topeka, N.D., (re: George Crawford).

Armstrong, Linda. *Tanya's Desert Star*, St. Petersburg, Florida, 1997.

Asmussen, Mable, Ed. *The History of Palisade, Colorado*, Typescript, Palisade, 1963.

Athearn, Robert G. *The Coloradans*, Albuquerque, New Mexico, 1976.

Austin, Hazel Baker. *Surface Creek Country* (2nd Ed.), Cedaredge, 1997.

Baird, J. Kenneth. "The Ku Klux Klan in Grand Junction, 1924 – 1927," *Journal of the Western Slope*, Winter 1989.

Barcus, Earlynne, and Irma Harrison. *Echoes of a Dream*, Fruita, 1980.

Barnett, Peggy. "Crawford: A Good Little Town," *Journal of the Western Slope*, Spring 1987.

Baver, William, James Ozment and John Willard. *Colorado Postal History: The Post Offices*, Denver, 1975.

Bergner, Merton N. "The Development of Fruita and the Lower Valley of the Colorado River from 1884 to 1937," unpublished M.A. thesis, University of Colorado, Boulder, 1937.

Bishop, Laura. (re: Rivera's Exploration), *Grand Junction Daily Sentinel*, April 13, 1991.

Bowman, Barbara. "The Peach Festival, 1887 – 1909: A Celebration of the Land," *Journal of the Western Slope*, Fall 1987.

Bowman, George W. "Some of the High Spots in the Life and Experiences of George W. Bowman," *History of Palisade* (unpublished collection, 1941), Palisade Branch Library.

Boyd, Natasha. *Ola Anfenson: Pioneer Photographer*, Albuquerque, New Mexico, 1997.

Brown, Donald A. "Emmett Elizondo: Sheepman Extraordinary," Wichita, Kansas. *Wichita Farm Credit Letter*, reprinted in *The Historian*, Fruita, 2002.

Brown, Larry. "Al Look," *Grand Junction Daily Sentinel*, June 11, 1972.

Brumgardt, John A. and George A. Woolsey, Jr. "Failure in Eden: The Cross Orchards Ranch, 1909-1923," *Colorado Heritage*, #4, 1984.

Bunte, William Kirk. "A History of Rapid Creek," *Journal of the Western Slope*, Fall 1994.

Buys, Christian J. "Chinese in Early Grand Junction," *Journal of the Western Slope*, Spring 1997.

Casebier, Caleb. "The Toughest Game Warden of All," *Colorado Outdoors*, Jan. – Feb. 1987.

Castle, Phil, "Campus Life," *Life and Times in Western Colorado*, March/April 2000.

Centennial-Bicentennial Brochure Committee. *Hotchkiss and Crawford 1881-1910*, Hotchkiss, 1976.

Chavez, Fray Angelo (Tr.) *The Dominguez-Escalante Journal*, Provo, Utah, 1976.

Chenoweth, William L. "Book Mountains – Book Cliffs: Historical Observations, 1853-1875," unpublished paper, Museum of Western Colorado, N.D.

_____. "The Riggs Hill and Dinosaur Hill Sites, Mesa County, Colorado," in Walter Averett, Ed., *Paleontology and Geology of the Dinosaur Triangle*, Grand Junction, 1987.

_____. *Observations at Crossings of the Colorado River in the Grand Valley, 1842-1879*, (Riverfront Foundation), Grand Junction, 1997.

Clark, Carrie. "The Bug House: History of the Colorado Insectary, Palisade, Colorado," *Journal of the Western Slope*, Summer 1999.

Coal Age Magazine, January 1949.

Cook, Bruce. *Dalton Trumbo*, New York, New York, 1977.

Correll, Hilary. "War Relief Efforts of Mesa County During the Second World War," *Journal of the Western Slope*, Summer 1996.

Coxsell, Andrew. "The Electric Boy Genius," *GQ Magazine*, December 2002.

Delta County Independent, April 19, 1918.

Denhart, Robert M. *Foundation Sires of the American Quarterhourse*, Lexington, KY, N.D.

Denver Post, "Dalton Trumbo, Film Master, Dies," September 4, 1976.

Dougherty, Deborah. *Delta, Colorado: The First 100 Years*, Delta, 1981.

DuPont Magazine, September 1952 (re: Audin)

Farmer, Louis C. *Snowbound in the High Rockies and Other True Short Stories*, Denver, 1985.

Ferrier, Mamie. *Valley Roads and Mountain Trails: Life on the Evening Side of the West Elks*, Crawford, 1998.

Ferrier, Mamie and George Sibley. *Long Horns and Short Tales*, Hotchkiss, 1977.

Fishell, Dave. *A Spirit of Charity 1896-1996: St. Mary's Hospital*, Grand Junction, 1996.

_____. *The Grand Heritage*, Norfolk, Virginia, 1985.

Foutz, Dell R. *The Geology of Colorado*, Grand Junction, 1978.

Gear, Ernest. *Eyewitness*, Collbran, 1990.

Golden, David. "William J. Moyer: The Rise and Fall of a Small Town Progressive in Western Colorado," *Journal of the Western Slope*, Summer 1995.

Grand Junction Daily Sentinel, 1908 – 1957.

_____. June 25, 1965 (re: Job Corps).

Grand Junction News. "Mesa Lakes Resort," June 13, 1891.

_____. "Park Opera House," June 25, 1891.

_____. "Old Actor Buried Here," February 22, 1892.

Grand Junction Star. "Crawford," January 27, 1891.

Grand Valley Gazette. "A Pioneer Tale," May, 1975.

Gregory, Lee. *Colorado Scenic Guide: Southern Region,* Boulder, 1985.

Harrison, Irma. "The Shepherd," *Lower Valley Heritage,* No. 8, 1979.

Haskell, Charles. *History of Mesa County,* Grand Junction, 1915.

Haynes, Dave. "Carving a Niche," *Grand Junction Daily Sentinel,* March 27, 1993.

Herrera, Liz. "Hispanic People of Grand Junction," *Journal of the Western Slope,* Fall 1991.

Herron, Lydia, Ed. *Spirit of Pioneer Women,* engagement calendars, Grand Junction, 1998, 1999, 2000.

Hyde, Helen. Unpublished manuscript, Paonia, 1983.

Izienicki, Jeffrey. "A Study of the Retolaza Boarding House and its Role in the Life of a Basque Itinerant Sheepherder," *Journal of the Western Slope,* Winter 1992.

Jones, Elaine Hale. "A Tribute to Muriel Marshall," *Montrose Daily Press,* April 13, 2000.

Kania, Alan J. *John Otto and the Colorado National Monument,* Boulder, 1984.

_____. *John Otto: Trials and Trails,* Niwot, 1996.

Keener, James and Cristine. *Colorado 141: Unaweep to Uravan,* Grand Junction, 1988.

_____. *Grand Mesa: World's Largest Flat Top Mountain,* Grand Junction, 1989.

Kessler, Ron. *Old Spanish Trail North Branch and its Travelers,* Santa Fe, New Mexico, 1998.

Klemenic, John. *Cameo: Birth, Life and Death of a Small Mining Community,* Palisade, 1998.

Kyle, E. Taped interview with Jean Urrity, March 10, 1975, in Loyd Files Research Center, Museum of Western Colorado.

Lemaster, Pat and Alice Wright. (re: Dr. Gould) *Daily Sentinel,* November 20, 1977.

MacKendrick, Donald A. "Thunder West of the Divide: James W. Bucklin, Western Colorado Utopian Reformer," *Essays and Monographs in Colorado History,* Denver, 1984.

_____. "The Roan Creek Toll Road," *Journal of the Western Slope,* Winter 1987.

_____. "Cesspools, Alkalai and White Lily Soap: The Grand Junction Indian School, 1886-1911," *Journal of the Western Slope,* Summer 1993.

_____. "Splendid Public Temples: The Development of Libraries in Mesa County, Colorado, 1892-1997," *Journal of the Western Slope,* Spring 1997.

Marshall, Muriel. *Island in the Sky: The Story of Grand Mesa*, Ouray, 1999.

_____. *Red Hole in Time*, College Station, Texas, 1988.

_____. "Sky Island: Land's End Ladder," *Delta County Independent*, October 26, 1996.

_____. *Where Rivers Meet*, College Station, Texas, 1996.

_____. *The Awesome 'Dobe Badlands*, Ouray, 2000.

Martin, Edward. *Psychology of Funeral Service*, Grand Junction, 1950.

McCall, Laura. "In the Spirit of Public Service: Leslie J. Savage of Western Colorado," *Journal of the Western Slope*, Winter 1990.

McCrenor, Emma. *Mesa County, Colorado: A 100-Year History*, Grand Junction, 1986.

McCulloch, David. *Truman*, New York, 1992.

McGuire, William L. and Charles Teed. *The Fruit Belt Route*, Grand Junction, 1981.

Mease, Janet. "The Grand Junction Town Company and the Land Dispute with William Keith," *Journal of the Western Slope*, Summer 1986.

Mihelich, John. *The Town of Welcome*, unpublished paper for Western State College, Hotchkiss, 1985.

Minor, Will C. *Footprints in the Trail*, Chicago, IL, 1950.

Mitford, Jessica. *The American Way of Death*, New York, 1963.

Moloney, Michael. "A History of the Palisade Wine Industry," *Journal of the Western Slope*, Spring 1996.

Moores, Jean. *Gateway/Unaweep Canyon at Some Point in Time*, Decorah, Iowa, 2000.

Morgan, Helen. *Looking Back on Delta County*. Vol. I and II, Delta, 1979 and 1980.

Morrow, Doug. "Champion Tree Receives Certification," *Mountain Valley News*, April 10, 1995.

Morton, Louis G. *Mesa College: The First Fifty Years*, Grand Junction, 1982.

Musser, Eda Baker, *Trails and Trials*, Delta, 1986.

Nelson, Jack. "North Branch of the 'Old Spanish Trail,'" *Journal of the Western Slope*, Fall 1996.

Noel, Thomas J. *Buildings of Colorado*, New York, 1997.

North Fork Times, December 10, 1975, (re: Tony Garcia).

Orr, Elmer. *Experience in Lieu of Education*, Montrose, 1984.

Ott, Richard, Ed. *When the River Was Grand*, Palisade, 1976.

Ozbun, Albert. *A Glade Park History Remembered*, Grand Junction, 1983.

Pabor, William Edgar. *Colorado as an Agricultural State: Its Farms, Fields and Garden Lands*, New York, 1883.

_____. *A Manual of Information*, Denver, 1883.

Page, Jean. *From Hoof to Wheel: The History of Grand Junction, Colorado*, Albuquerque, New Mexico, 1992.

Palisade Tribune, 1905-1928.

Peterson, Yvonne. Scrapbook, Lower Valley Heritage Chapter, Fruita, N.D.

Pitts, Reuben A. *The Bulls and the Bees: The Facts of Life in the Plateau Valley*, Grand Junction, 1997.

Pratiyer, Sarah and Armand DeBeque. *History of Roan Creek and DeBeque, 1884–1984*, DeBeque, 1984.

Progressive Men of Western Colorado, Chicago, 1905.

Rader, Gertrude. "The New Deal Program as Seen from Loma" (compiled from Mesa County oral history tapes by L. L. Haseman), *Journal of the Western Slope*, Fall 1987.

_____. (as told to L.L. Haseman), "Community Development and Historical Events," *Journal of the Western Slope*, Winter 1991.

Rait, Mary. "Development of Grand Junction and the Colorado River Valley to Palisade from 1881 to 1931, Parts I & II," *Journal of the Western Slope*, Summer and Autumn 1988.

Reddin, Paul. *Wild West Shows*, Urbana, IL, 1999.

Reyher, Ken. *Antoine Robidoux and Fort Uncompahgre*, Ouray 1998.

Righdenour, Mabyl. "Pipe Line School, Glade Park," *Lower Valley Heritage*, No. 3, 1977.

Rockwell, Wilson M. "The Fruit Utopia of the North Fork of the Gunnison," *Colorado Magazine,* May, 1938.

_____. *New Frontiers*, Denver, 1945.

_____. *Uncompahgre Country*, Denver, 1965.

Roeber, Clinton. *West Elk Tales*, Paonia, 1985.

Rolland, Megan. "Junction Bridge Partners Place 25th in World," *Grand Junction Free Press*, August 7, 2003.

Saccomanno Research Institute Papers: "Bibliography of Geno Saccomanno" and "Curriculum Vitae: Geno Saccomanno," N.D.

Sauer, Rachel. "Hollywood Ten Legend Found Fame in Tinseltown and Infamy in Grand Junction," *Grand Junction Daily Sentinel,* December 2, 2000.

Scher, Zeke. "The Arches of Rattlesnake Canyon," *Denver Post Empire Magazine*, August 10, 1980.

Schulte, Steven C. *Wayne Aspinall and the Shaping of the American West*, Boulder, 2002.

Seely, Eleanor. *A History of Our School: Lincoln Orchard Mesa*, Grand Junction, N.D.

Schwochow, Stephen D. *Mineral Resources Survey of Mesa County,* Denver, 1978.

Shaw, Luella. *True History of Some of the Pioneers of Colorado,* Hotchkiss, 1909.

Silbernagel, Bob. (re: Wilson Rockwell). *Grand Junction Daily Sentinel*, October 22, 1993.

_____. "Saccomanno Stance on Radon Supported," *Grand Junction Daily Sentinel*, December 21, 1994.

206

_____. "Porcupine Quills Pricked Interest in Medicine, Cancer Research," *Grand Junction Daily Sentinel,* March 26, 1995.

Simmons, Craig and Adam McBride. "Biography of Frank Dean," unpublished paper, Museum of Western Colorado, N.D.

Smith, Jeannette, "Walter Walker and His Fight Against Socialism," *Journal of the Western Slope,* Fall 1997.

Steinel, Alvin T. *History of Agriculture in Colorado,* Fort Collins, 1926.

Stewart, Ada Hall. "Early History of Plateau Valley, Colorado, and Pioneer Life of the First Settlers, As Related by Them or Their Relatives," (Mesa, 1931), *Journal of the Western Slope,* Fall 2000.

Stewart, George. *The Sowing and the Reaping: A Western Reflection,* Caldwell, ID, 1970.

Stickney, Dane. "Jurassic Exhibit Added to Dinosaur Journey," *Grand Junction Free Press,* June 20, 2003.

Sullivan, Nancy L. "DeBeque's Odd Fellows' Hall," *Shale Country,* Summer 1983.

Sundal, David. "Aviation in Mesa County: A Brief Survey," *Mesa County Historical Society Bulletin,* March/April 1999.

Tennent, William L. "The Day Buffalo Bill Came to Town," *Museum Journal,* 1985, reprinted in *Journal of the Western Slope,* Summer 2000.

Thrapp, Dan L. *Encyclopedia of Frontier Biography,* Glendale, California, 1988.

Tope, Richard E. "Objective History: Grand Junction Colorado Part I," *Journal of the Western Slope,* Winter 1995.

Trumbo, Dalton. "About the Play," in Program Notes for "The Biggest Thief in Town."

_____. *Additional Dialogue: Letters of Dalton Trumbo 1942-1962,* New York, 1970.

Tyson, Monk and Parma (re: Charles Weddle), *Denver Post,* January 12, 1958.

Underwood, Kathleen. *Town Building on the Colorado Frontier,* Albuquerque, New Mexico, 1987.

Vanderwilt, John W. *Mineral Resources of Colorado,* Denver, 1947.

Wallace, William. *Antoine Robidoux, 1794-1860: A Biography of a Western Venturer,* Los Angeles, 1953.

Wetzel, James K. *A Spirit Returns: Delta County, Colorado: A Pictorial History,* Virginia Beach, Virginia, 2003.

Wheeler, David L. "The Far Country: Wild Horses, Public Lands, and the Little Book Cliffs of Colorado," *Journal of the Western Slope,* Winter/Spring 1998.

Williams, Florence. "Town Wants End of Rainbows' Visit," *Albuquerque Journal,* July 2, 1992.

Wills, Lila M. *Tale of the Serpent,* Fruita, 1980.

Wood, Nancy. "America's Most Radioactive City," *McCall's Magazine,* September 1970.

Woodruff, Phillip. "A Collection of Notes and History on Enos T. Hotchkiss," unpublished paper for Western State College, Hotchkiss, 1984.

Works Projects Administration Writers' Program. *Colorado: Guide to the Highest State,* New York, 1941.

Wright, Alice. "A Sheepman Speaks," *Grand Junction Daily Sentinel,* February 13, 1972.

_____. "Who Was W.Z. Moyer?" *Grand Junction Daily Sentinel,* January 15, 1972.

Young, Helen Hawxhurst. *The Skin and Bones of Plateau Valley History,* Grand Junction, 1976.

Young, Leslie A. *The Grand Junction News, 1882-1883,* unpublished M.A. thesis, University of Utah, Salt Lake City, 1987.

Young, Robert G. and Joan W. *Land of Geology and Wildflowers,* Grand Junction, 1984.

Zimmerman, Harold. "Harvesting Peaches with German Prisoners of War," *Journal of the Western Slope,* Winter 1987.

INDEX

G
R
A
N
D

M
E
S
A

C
O
U
N
T
R
Y

Thunder Mountain Lives Tonight! 94
Todd, Thomas 78-79
Trees, Largest 26
Trujillo, Juanita 134
Truman, Harry 39-40
Trumbo, Dalton 145-146

Uintah Railroad 23
Unaweep Canyon 18
Uncompahgre River 9-10
Unidentified Flying Objects 158
Urrity, Jean 52-53
Unser, Louis 132
Ute Indians 2-3, 16

Van Dusen , Robert 93
Veterans Administration Hospital 177

Wade, Samuel 62, 67
Walker, Walter 78-79, 84-85, 128
Walsh, Charles 128
Warner, M. Rush 62
Weddle, Charles L. 186-187
Welcome 73-74
Western Colorado Air Force Association 162
Western Colorado Center for the Arts 177
Western Colorado Commercial Travelers' Association 163
Western Colorado Math and Science Center 112-113
Wetzel, David 24
Wheeler, David L. 50
Whitewater 142
Whitman, Marcus 14
Wild Horses 49-51
Wills, Lila 71
Witchel, Isaac 90
Works Progress Administration 75
Wright, Silas 91
Wubben, Horace and Irene 108-109

Yeager, Charles 130

Zimmerman, Bob and Mary 185